PALEO EFFECT

150 All-Natural Recipes for a Grain-Free, Dairy-Free Lifestyle

Meghan Little and Angel Ayala Torres

Skyhorse Publishing

Skyhorse Publishing books may be purchased in bulk at special discounts for sales promotion, corporate gifts, fund-raising, or educational purposes. Special editions can also be created to specifications. For details, contact the Special Sales Department, Skyhorse Publishing, 307 West 36th Street, 11th Floor, New York, NY 10018 or info@skyhorsepublishing.com.

Skyhorse® and Skyhorse Publishing® are registered trademarks of Skyhorse Publishing, Inc. ®, a Delaware corporation.

www.skyhorsepublishing.com

10 9 8 7 6 5 4 3 2 1

Library of Congress Cataloging-in-Publication Data is available on file.

ISBN: 978-1-62636-162-1

Printed in China

This book is dedicated to the many people who have lived, dealt, and battled with health issues, as well as our friends and most importantly, our families, who have raised us with an appreciation, love and respect for food.

You are the reason we have had the opportunity to make this book and we personally want to say thank you for your time, thoughts, energy and support.

MEET THE AUTHORS

We met in March of 2010 and instantly fell in love. As many of you know and understand, it is quite difficult to mesh diet lifestyles, especially cross-culturally. We had spent so much time together that we had really started to let our health deteriorate and finally came to the decision to do something about it. We started barefoot running in the summer of 2010, and after many conversations about our nutrition, and after many books and research, we found the Paleo Diet. The night we finished the book is the night we cleaned out the pantry and changed our lives forever. Within a month, we both lost excess weight, the migraines that had plagued Angel were gone, and the joint issues and sleep insomnia had vanished from our lives. No more doctor appointments, no more medications. We have both been pill free for over 2 years. We loved it so much, we decided to start a website and blog, www.paleoeffect.com, to share our journey and our recipes with others and build a community for a healthier and happier lifestyle.

As a new practitioner, you will find that it is quite an adjustment for your body when transitioning to the Paleo Diet. It takes about 2-3 weeks for your body to cleanse and adjust, and this is normal. You will find that if you stick with it for 30 days, you will become an advocate. For more information, success stories, and a fantastic community of helpful, Paleo enthusiasts, visit our blog, Facebook, Pinterest, Twitter, Google Plus, or Instagram for more information!

It has been a truly amazing journey and we can't wait for you to join us!

SIDES #102

PORK #138

WILD CAUGHT #156

GRASS FED #126

CAGE FREE #146

SWEETS #169

INTRODUCTION TO PALEO

The Paleolithic (Paleo) Diet (also popularly referred to as the Caveman Diet) is a nutritional plan based on the ancient diet of Paleolithic man, namely consisting of fruits, vegetables, nuts, and wild-caught animal proteins. "Paleolithic" refers to a period roughly 2.5 million years in duration that ended around 10,000 years ago with the development of agriculture. Centered on pre-agricultural foods, the "contemporary" Paleolithic Diet consists mainly of meats, fish, vegetables, fruits, roots, oils, and nuts—and excludes grains, legumes, dairy products, processed foods, and refined sugars. That's right. No grains, dairy, beans, or highly processed sugars or oils of any kind. It sounds difficult, but if you give it a chance and experience it, you'll feel better than you thought you could. You'll feel lighter on your feet . . . You'll sleep better . . . You can relax and just eat without feeling guilty! The Paleo Diet is ideal for individuals with gastrointestinal problems, lactose intolerance, celiac disease, autoimmune diseases, diabetes, as well as a variety of other health issues. If you'd like to learn more, we recommend reading Robb Wolf's *The Paleo Solution* to dive further into the science behind the success and help you understand how the Paleo lifestyle can work for you!

QUICK PALEO HOW-TO GUIDE

We've all been there. You are trying to start a new lifestyle, change your diet, and change your life, but you don't know where to start. This quick reference guide will help you make quick decisions for good foods to eat by providing a few examples (it does not list every single food in that group; again, it's a quick guide). If you want to learn more about all of the good and the bad, see our Dos and Don'ts section!

GOOD FOODS TO EAT

MEATS

Beef, Pork, Lamb, Veal, Rabbit, Goat, Sheep, Bison, Deer

Basically, if you can catch it, you can eat it. We recommend that you try to buy all grass fed and antibiotic free if possible.

POULTRY

Chicken, Turkey, Duck, Quail, Goose

We recommend that you try to buy all free range and antibiotic free if possible.

SHELLFISH

Shrimp, Scallops, Clams, Oysters, Mussels, Lobster, Crab

We recommend that you try to buy all wild caught and antibiotic free if possible.

FISH

Salmon, Trout, Tuna, Bass, Halibut, Sole, Haddock, Tilapia

We recommend that you try to buy all wild caught and antibiotic free if possible.

FATS

Coconut Oil, Avocado Oil, Fat from Protein/Lard, Olive Oil, Nut Butters, Nut Oils, Fruit Oils, Flower Oils (though keep the safflower and sunflower to a minimum; we want the least amount of processing possible)

EGGS

We recommend free range or cage free and antibiotic free.

VEGETABLES

Tomatoes, Peppers, Onions, Asparagus, Cucumbers, Avocados, Cabbage, Broccoli, Squash, Mushrooms, Anything Green or Colorful

Steer clear of vegetables that you cannot eat raw.

LEAFY GREENS

Lettuce, Spinach, Chard, Watercress, Endive, Arugula

You can eat as many leafy greens as you want! No matter what kind!

ROOT VEGETABLES

Carrots, Beets, Radishes, Yams, Parsnips, Sweet Potatoes

We eat root vegetables usually earlier in the day. If you are looking for rapid weight loss, limit this section.

NUTS AND SEEDS

Almonds, Hazelnuts, Pecans, Walnuts, Brazil Nuts, Pistachios

Limit your intake of nuts to 1–2 oz per day. See our Portions Cheat Sheet on our blog for more information!

FRUITS

Berries, Melons, Grapes, Plums, Peaches, Apples, Bananas

All fruits are OK. Limit these if you are looking for rapid weight loss. See our Glycemic Index on our blog for more information on high-sugar fruits.

HERBS AND SPICES

Ginger, Garlic, Parsley, Sage, Chilies, Vanilla, Mint, Basil

Learning how to use spices properly will really help you love your foods even more!

PALEO DOS AND DON'TS

The Paleo Diet solution mimics our hunter and gatherer ancestors. So if you can find or kill it in nature, you can eat it, essentially. We've taken the time to outline in greater detail the rules of the road for successful Paleo eating. For even more information, go to our blog at www.paleoeffect.com!

EAT YOUR VEGETABLES

Eat as many fresh or frozen vegetables as you want. Go organic and live it up. And don't be shy; these can be eaten raw or cooked, any way you like!

NO DAIRY

Nope. Did you know that humans are the only species to continue to drink milk after infancy? Did you know that dairy is an immune system stressor and everyone is allergic to cow dairy to some extent? The bottom line? Avoid all dairy. This includes milk, butter, cream, yogurt, ice cream, cheese, etc.

GO CARNIVORE

Try to focus on moderate to high animal protein. Your body craves it and your waistline will thank you. I used to be vegetarian and I must tell you, after 20 years of not eating beef or pork, I feel better now than I ever did as a vegetarian. If you don't have serious PETA morals, go back to meat. And yes, that means even fattier cuts like bacon and ribs. We eat a variety of poultry, seafood, red meats, and eggs—all wild caught or grass fed (as the hormones will mess up your system … Have you seen how big kids are today?! Not. Natural.)

AVOID MOST STARCHES

No corn products, no potatoes, no rice, no breads. If you feel you need rice, try cauliflower. You can food-process it and spice it up to help you get over the hump. It's surprisingly good! The exceptions here are tubers like sweet potatoes, carrots, parsnips, and plantains; these are OK. Try to think "Can I eat it raw?" and if the answer is *yes*, then you can eat it on the Paleo Diet. See our recipes for other ways to mimic the foods you may miss (including cookies!).

NO PROCESSED FOODS

If it comes in the freezer section or in a box, you probably can't eat it, except for frozen vegetables and fruit. It is very important that you avoid nitrates and nitrites. So watch out for those (especially in things like bacon and sausage, as they make some that are grass fed and without nitrates).

OILS

Good oils to use (and use them plenty) include coconut (our favorite for cooking), palm, avocado, sesame, grape-seed, and olive oils. Avoid corn, cottonseed, peanut, soybean, rice bran, and wheat germ oils. Avoid any foods made with these oils (yes, that means foods like chips and mayo, whether they are organic or not). For more information on which oils to use and for what, see our Fats/Oils guide on Which to Eat and Which to Ditch on Facebook and Pinterest!

NO GRAINS

None. Nada. Not even corn (yes, corn is a grain). And I'll tell you why. Wheat has gluten and all grains have a very high glycemic index, which means that these foods carry sugar too rapidly into the bloodstream. For more details, read *The Paleo Solution* by Robb Wolf. He details in length the internal effects on your body of going Paleo, and it's really a fantastic read.

LEGUMES (BEANS, PEANUTS)

You might be thinking these are OK, but consider: Even though I can find it in nature, can I eat it raw? And the answer to legumes is no. Go ahead, eat a raw kidney bean and tell me if it's tasty. Prior to agriculture, legumes were very rare and were not a staple in our diets. They contain lectins, saponins, phytates, and protease inhibitors that are bad news for our hormonal and immune systems. See Robb's book again for more info. Many Paleo and Primal practitioners will bend this rule for peas and green beans, as they contain only trace amounts of anti-nutrients. We do not use them in our cooking often, but if you'd like to eat them from time to time, you should be OK, as long as you are not suffering from any health issues.

FRUITS AND FRUIT JUICES

We eat all the fruits we want, but again, if you are trying to lose a decent amount of weight, we recommend that you limit your intake, as fruits contain a lot of sugar. Remember, the sugar is natural, but it's still sugar! Go organic. If you are drinking juices, go for organic, not-from-concentrate, non-blends. If you are in for the weight loss, see our Glycemic Index on our blog at www.paleoeffect.com to see which fruits are higher and lower in sugar.

NUTS

If you can find it in nature, you can eat it. So cashews, pecans, almonds, walnuts, etc. are OK. They have essential oils, fats, and proteins that are good for you, but eat in moderation. The logic behind this is that nuts contain phytic acid (commonly found in grains and legumes), which interferes with enzymes we need to digest our food. Moderation is OK, but if you eat a lot, it can lead to mineral deficiencies like osteoporosis. Think Caveman: How many nuts could you find in nature, crack, and eat before you would give up? About a handful (1–2 ounces), I'm assuming, which is about right.

SALT

We prefer to use sea salt instead of iodized salt, as sea salt requires less processing. The key here is to note that regardless of the type of salt you choose to use, it should be used in moderation, as salt was not a common ingredient in the Paleo Diet.

BOOZE

Let's be honest. It's hard to give up the booze. But if you can't give it up, you can do it Paleo-style. We drink wine (as it is gluten free) that is organically grown and beer that is gluten free, or hard ciders. Some recommendations are Bard's (made from sorghum) and Woodchuck (made from apples). Robb Wolf also recommends what he calls the "NorCal" Margarita, which is made by combining soda water, lime, and 100% agave tequila. This is also something that we drink occasionally. If you have severe autoimmune disease or allergies, we have an alcohol guide on our blog that details the contents of each type of alcohol, so you can make the best choices for your body.

COFFEE AND TEA

You'll hear a wide variety of what to do with coffee and tea. We maintain that a little coffee or tea with caffeine is OK, but if you're drinking it all day, swap out the caffeine with some decaf.

NIX THE SUGARS

No soft drinks, no flavored drinks, no processed fruit snacks, etc. If you are not interested in weight loss, you can use some honey, coconut crystals, or pure cane sugar, but these should be used in moderation. And remember, if it comes ready-made, you probably shouldn't eat it.

PORTION CONTROL

Eat as much of these foods as you want! If you need to seriously lose some pounds, you may want to consider limiting your intake of fruits and nuts, but otherwise, go wild!

SUPPLEMENTS

These are not necessary, but Robb Wolf does make some recommendations in his book *The Paleo Solution* if you are interested in learning more.

EATING SCHEDULE

Don't keep a schedule. You should eat when you are hungry, and don't eat when you aren't. You will have days where you go all day with no food and others where you eat every few hours. This is normal. Just do what feels natural.

CHEATING

It is normal and OK to have a cheat every now and again. Just remember that cheating doesn't mean go out and eat 4 pizzas, drink a gallon of soda, and eat 6 packs of french fries. You can eat non-Paleo foods from time to time, but keep it under control. We like to reserve these moments for when we have parties or holidays, special occasions, and, at times, a little great, grass-fed cheese or butter.

ORGANIC VS. NON-ORGANIC

Trust me, we know that being Paleo is not always cheap or easy, especially if you have children. If you are in an area where organic is difficult to find, or choose not to go completely organic for other reasons, there are some guidelines that you should follow—*especially* if you have children. The guide below is based off of research from the Environmental Working Group (EWG) and categorizes the amounts of pesticides found in fruits and vegetables. Note that these were washed and, if applicable, peeled (i.e., bananas) before testing.

RED LIGHT!

Red means stop! Avoid eating these fruits and vegetables unless they are organic:

Peaches, Apples, Sweet Bell Peppers, Celery, Nectarines, Strawberries, Cherries, Carrots, Pears, Frozen Winter Squash

ORANGE LIGHT!

Orange . . . Well, it also means stop. The produce in this category is not quite as horrible as in the red light section, but still, go organic:

Spinach, Grapes, Lettuce, Green Beans, Hot Peppers, Cucumbers, Mushrooms, Cantaloupe, Oranges, Fresh Winter Squash

YELLOW LIGHT!

Yellow means proceed with caution. These foods absorb less chemicals, but are not perfect:

Applesauce, Raspberries, Plums, Grapefruit, Tangerines, Apple Juice, Honeydew Melon, Tomatoes, Sweet Potatoes, Watermelon, Cauliflower

GREEN LIGHT!

Green means go! The foods in this section contain very low amounts of contaminants:

Broccoli, Orange Juice, Blueberries, Papaya, Cabbage, Bananas, Kiwi, Canned Tomatoes, Sweet Peas, Asparagus, Mango, Canned Pears, Pineapple, Avocado, Onions

A GUIDE TO SEASONAL PRODUCE

Choosing seasonal fruits and vegetables can really save you money while practicing a Paleo lifestyle, but it's hard to know what's what and when to find it. If you have a local farmer's market, it makes it a little easier; basically anything that you can find there will be in season! But if you don't, or you live in a climate where it is cold more often than hot, then we hope this guide will help you figure out the basics. If you eat local or seasonal foods, they will taste better and make your dishes, your wallet, and your stomach happy! Note: the following is based on US growing seasons.

MONTH	PRODUCE
JANUARY	Avocado, Bell Pepper, Broccoli (and Broccoli Rabe), Brussels Sprouts, Cabbage, Carambola, Carrot, Cauliflower, Celery (and Celery Root), Cilantro, Chard, Chilies, Coconuts, Collard Greens, Cucumber, Eggplant, Fennel, Grapefruit, Green Onions, Guava, Kale, Leeks, Lemon, Lemongrass, Lettuce, Lime, Mandarin Oranges, Mushrooms, Okra, Onions, Oranges, Oregano, Papaya, Parsley, Passion Fruit, Peppers (sweet), Pomelos, Radish, Squash, Strawberries, Tangerines, Thyme, Tomatoes, Tomatillo, Zucchini
FEBRUARY	Bell Pepper, Broccoli (and Broccoli Rabe), Brussels Sprouts, Cabbage, Carambola, Carrot, Cauliflower, Celery (and Celery Root), Cilantro, Chard, Chilies, Coconuts, Collard Greens, Cucumber, Eggplant, Fennel, Grapefruit, Green Onions, Guava, Kale, Leeks, Lemon, Lemongrass, Lettuce, Lime, Mandarin Oranges, Mushrooms, Onions, Oranges, Oregano, Papaya, Parsley, Passion Fruit, Peppers (sweet), Pomelos, Radish, Spinach, Squash, Strawberries, Tangerines, Thyme, Tomatoes, Tomatillo, Zucchini
MARCH	Basil, Bell Pepper, Broccoli (and Broccoli Rabe), Brussels Sprouts, Cabbage, Cantaloupe, Carambola, Carrot, Cauliflower, Celery (and Celery Root), Cilantro, Chard, Chilies, Coconuts, Collard Greens, Cucumber, Eggplant, Fennel, Grapefruit, Green Onions, Guava, Kale, Leeks, Lemon, Lemongrass, Lettuce, Lime, Mandarin Oranges, Melon, Mushrooms, Onions, Oranges, Oregano, Papaya, Parsley, Passion Fruit, Peppers (sweet), Pineapple, Pomelos, Radish, Spinach, Squash, Strawberries, Tangerines, Thyme, Tomatoes, Tomatillo, Zucchini
APRIL	Artichoke, Asparagus, Basil, Bell Pepper, Blueberries, Broccoli (and Broccoli Rabe), Cabbage, Cantaloupe, Carrot, Cauliflower, Celery (and Celery Root), Cilantro, Chard, Chilies, Coconuts, Collard Greens, Cucumber, Eggplant, Fennel, Grapefruit, Green Onions, Guava, Kale, Leeks, Lemon, Lemongrass, Lettuce, Lime, Mandarin Oranges, Melon, Mushrooms, Onions, Oranges, Oregano, Papaya, Parsley, Peppers (sweet), Pineapple, Pomelos, Radish, Rhubarb, Squash, Strawberries, Tangerines, Thyme, Tomatoes, Tomatillo, Watermelon, Zucchini
MAY	Apricot, Artichoke, Asparagus, Basil, Bell Pepper, Blueberries, Broccoli (and Broccoli Rabe), Cabbage, Cantaloupe, Carrot, Cauliflower, Celery (and Celery Root), Cilantro, Chard, Chilies, Coconuts, Collard Greens, Cucumber, Eggplant, Fennel, Grapefruit, Green Onions, Guava, Jackfruit, Kale, Leeks, Lemon, Lemongrass, Lettuce, Lime, Mandarin Oranges, Mango, Melon, Mushrooms, Onions, Oranges, Oregano, Papaya, Parsley, Peppers (sweet), Pineapple, Radish, Rhubarb, Squash, Strawberries, Tangerines, Thyme, Tomatoes, Tomatillo, Watermelon, Zucchini

JUNE	Avocado, Apricot, Basil, Bell Pepper, Blackberries, Blueberries, Cabbage, Cantaloupe, Carrot, Celery (and Celery Root), Cherries, Chilies, Coconuts, Cucumber, Dragon Fruit, Eggplant, Fennel, Grapefruit, Green Onions, Guava, Jackfruit, Leeks, Lemon, Lime, Lychee, Mandarin Oranges, Mango, Melon, Mushrooms, Nectarines, Onions, Oregano, Papaya, Parsley, Passion Fruit, Peaches, Peppers (sweet), Radish, Squash, Strawberries, Thyme, Tomatoes, Tomatillo, Watermelon, Zucchini
JULY	Avocado, Apricot, Basil, Bell Pepper, Blackberries, Cantaloupe, Cherries, Coconuts, Dragon Fruit, Figs, Green Onions, Guava, Jackfruit, Kiwi, Leeks, Lemon, Lime, Longan, Mango, Melon, Mushrooms, Nectarines, Onions, Oregano, Papaya, Parsley, Passion Fruit, Peaches, Peppers (sweet), Plums, Raspberries, Watermelon
AUGUST	Avocado, Asian Pear, Apricot, Basil, Carambola, Cherries, Chilies, Coconuts, Dragon Fruit, Figs, Grapes, Green Onions, Guava, Jackfruit, Kiwi, Leeks, Lemon, Lime, Longan, Mango, Mushrooms, Nectarines, Okra, Onions, Oregano, Papaya, Parsley, Passion Fruit, Peaches, Plums, Raspberries
SEPTEMBER	Apples, Avocado, Asian Pear, Basil, Carambola, Chilies, Coconuts, Dragon Fruit, Eggplant, Fennel, Figs, Grapefruit, Grapes, Green Onions, Guava, Jackfruit, Leeks, Lemon, Lemongrass, Lime, Mango, Mushrooms, Okra, Onions, Oregano, Papaya, Parsley, Passion Fruit, Persimmon, Pomegranate, Pumpkin, Quinces, Squash, Strawberries, Sweet Potato, Tangerines, Thyme, Tomato, Tomatillo, Zucchini
OCTOBER	Apples, Avocado, Asian Pear, Basil, Bell Pepper, Broccoli (and Broccoli Rabe), Carambola, Chilies, Coconuts, Cranberries, Cucumber, Dragon Fruit, Eggplant, Fennel, Grapefruit, Green Onions, Guava, Jackfruit, Leeks, Lemon, Lemongrass, Lime, Mandarin Oranges, Mushrooms, Okra, Onions, Oranges, Oregano, Papaya, Parsley, Passion Fruit, Peppers (sweet), Persimmon, Pomegranate, Pumpkin, Quinces, Radish, Squash, Strawberries, Sweet Potato, Tangerines, Thyme, Tomato, Tomatillo, Zucchini
NOVEMBER	Apples, Avocado, Asian Pear, Basil, Bell Pepper, Broccoli (and Broccoli Rabe), Brussels Sprouts, Cabbage, Carambola, Carrot, Cauliflower, Celery (and Celery Root), Cilantro, Chard, Chilies, Coconuts, Collard Greens, Cranberries, Cucumber, Dragon Fruit, Eggplant, Fennel, Grapefruit, Green, Onions, Guava, Jackfruit, Kale, Leeks, Lemon, Lemongrass, Lettuce, Lime, Mandarin Oranges, Mushrooms, Okra, Onions, Oranges, Oregano, Papaya, Parsley, Passion Fruit, Peppers (sweet), Persimmon, Pomegranate, Pumpkin, Quinces, Radish, Squash, Strawberries, Sweet Potato, Tangerines, Thyme, Tomato, Tomatillo, Zucchini
DECEMBER	Avocado, Bell Pepper, Broccoli (and Broccoli Rabe), Brussels Sprouts, Cabbage, Carambola, Carrot, Cauliflower, Celery (and Celery Root), Cilantro, Chard, Chilies, Coconuts, Collard Greens, Cranberries, Cucumber, Eggplant, Fennel, Grapefruit, Green Onions, Guava, Kale, Leeks, Lemon, Lemongrass, Lettuce, Lime, Mandarin Oranges, Mushrooms, Okra, Onions, Oranges, Oregano, Papaya, Parsley, Passion Fruit, Peppers (sweet), Persimmon, Pomegranate, Pomelos, Radish, Squash, Strawberries, Sweet Potato, Tangerines, Thyme, Tomato, Tomatillo, Zucchini

GENERAL TIPS AND TRICKS

- All of the protein used in our recipes should be thawed and raw, unless noted specifically. You will find that if you use raw ingredients, the recipes will turn out to spec. If not, we make no guarantees!

- In each recipe, we use grass-fed meat, nitrate-free pork, wild-caught seafood, and cage-free poultry. We recommend buying antibiotic-free protein kinds if you can't find these in your local grocery store. The less hormones and chemicals that you ingest, the better.

- We also use fresh herbs for all recipes unless noted otherwise. Again, you can use dried, but remember that you will not need as much dried as fresh. If you choose to do this, we can't guarantee the measurements.

- We also always use freshly ground black pepper. Not the stuff that comes in the shaker from your local grocery store. Buy a grinder. It tastes different and you'll thank us later. All of our recipes are made with coarse sea salt as well.

- If you are looking for substitutes, visit our website www.paleoeffect.com.

- We like to use thick, full-fat coconut milk for all of our recipes. It has a better consistency and sets up better than watery or low-fat types. If you are using the store-bought coconut milk, make sure that there are no fillers, such as guar gum or xanthan gum.

- One vanilla bean is equal to one teaspoon of vanilla extract. So if you don't have vanilla beans, no worries, just use the extract.

- With all references to baking powder, please note that we use the aluminum-free type.

DICTIONARY OF UNCOMMON INGREDIENTS

When cooking Paleo, you may run into some ingredients that you may not know. To make it easy, we've added this glossary of ingredients to help you understand these new food items. If you can't find them in your local health food store, they are available to buy online.

ARROWROOT POWDER

Arrowroot is a starch obtained from the rootstock of tropical plants. It has no real flavor, so if you choose not to use it, it will not affect the flavor of any of the recipes in this book, only the texture. We use it primarily as a thickener for baked goods, soups, and sauces. If you prefer, you can use coconut flour instead. You will probably need to use more of it, and it may affect the texture, but it could work OK if you want to thicken a recipe and don't have arrowroot powder.

COCONUT AMINOS

Coconut aminos is a raw, soy-free alternative to soy sauce. It is made from coconut tree sap and is fermented with sun-dried sea salt, containing up to 14 times the amino acid content of soy. We use this in place of soy sauce. If you can't find any, you can use wheat-free tamari sauce as well if you can tolerate a little soy.

COCONUT CRYSTALS

Coconut crystals (i.e., coconut sugar, coconut palm sugar, or coco sap sugar) are produced from the sap of cut flower buds of the coconut palm. They taste a little like a light brown sugar and have been used as a sweetener in Southeast Asian regions for thousands of years. We use this in place of traditional sugar, but if you can't get any, you can use raw sugarcane or honey in place of this.

COCONUT VINEGAR

Coconut vinegar is made from the sap of the coconut tree. It is tapped, collected, then allowed to naturally ferment—raw, unfiltered, and unheated—for about 45-60 days. It tastes just like white vinegar, contains no added sugar, and requires no preservatives.

SLURRY

A slurry is a mixture of starch and liquid that is used to thicken a recipe. For the purposes of this book, it is a mixture of arrowroot and water. We mix the arrowroot with water before adding it to a recipe in order to keep the starchy arrowroot from clumping up and creating balls of starch. When you make a slurry first, you'll ensure a smooth consistency throughout.

THE BASICS

Adobo Seasoning • Mayonnaise • Breadcrumbs • BBQ Dry Rub Seasoning
Culantro Y Achiote Seasoning • Taco Seasoning • Sweet Chili Sauce • Balsamic Glaze
Refrigerator Dill Pickles • Don Ayala's Sofrito

ADOBO SEASONING

1 ½ Tbsp Sea Salt	½ tsp Oregano	⅛ tsp Turmeric
¼ tsp Garlic Powder	¼ tsp Black Pepper	

Combine all ingredients.

This recipe is Vegan

MAYONNAISE

1 cup Grape-Seed Oil	1 Egg Yolk	½ Tbsp Coconut Vinegar
1 Egg	1 Tbsp Lemon Juice	¼ tsp Sea Salt
	½ tsp Ground Mustard	

Let everything come to room temperature. You *must* do this or we can't guarantee it will turn out. Trust it; we've all failed a million times because of this. Blend the egg, egg yolk, mustard, and salt together. You can do this with a whisk, hand mixer, or blender, but we use our food processor, because it is fantastic and we love that thing. In a separate bowl, whisk together the lemon and vinegar. Add half to the eggs, whisk or blend, and set the other half aside.

Slowly add in the oil, a few drops at a time, and we mean a *slow* stream. *Drops* if you are whisking. Go slower than you think you need to until the liquid begins to thicken.

Once half of the oil is added, you can add the other half of the lemon mixture. Then whisk or add in the rest of the oil in a slow but steady stream.

Leave this at room temperature for 1–2 hours, then you can refrigerate for up to one week. Check your eggs' expiration date as well; you'll have to factor that in.

Tip You can use olive oil too, but it has an olive oil flavor, whereas grape-seed oil does not.

This recipe is Vegetarian

BREADCRUMBS

½ cup Almond Flour

¼ cup Golden Flaxseed Meal

1 tsp Garlic Powder

½ tsp Onion Powder

½ tsp Thyme

½ tsp Oregano

1 ½ tsp Sea Salt

½ tsp Black Pepper

Optional: 1 Tbsp Arrowroot Powder

Combine all ingredients and use as you would breadcrumbs.

Note You can use regular flaxseed meal if you want, but it will taste more like wheat bread.

Tip The arrowroot is optional. It will help bind the ingredients together but is not necessary for the taste of the dish, only the texture.

This recipe is Vegan

BBQ DRY RUB SEASONING

½ Tbsp Cumin	½ Tbsp Cayenne Powder	½ cup Coconut Crystals
1 Tbsp Garlic Powder	1 Tbsp Sea Salt	1 Tbsp Adobo Seasoning
1 Tbsp Onion Powder	1 Tbsp Black Pepper	(see page 14)
½ Tbsp Chili Powder	½ Tbsp Paprika	

Combine all ingredients.

This recipe is Vegan

CULANTRO Y ACHIOTE SEASONING

1 Tbsp Sea Salt	1 tsp Garlic Powder	¼ tsp Cumin
1 Tbsp Annatto Seeds	½ tsp Onion Powder	¼ tsp Culantro
2 tsp Chicken Bouillon	½ tsp Oregano	

Combine all ingredients.

Tip This is a popular seasoning in Puerto Rican cooking.
If you can't find culantro, you can use cilantro.

TACO SEASONING

2 tsp Chili Powder	½ tsp Black Pepper	¼ tsp Cumin
1 tsp Onion Flakes	¼ tsp Garlic Powder	¼ tsp Coriander
½ tsp Paprika	¼ tsp Red Pepper Flakes	*Optional*: 1 Tbsp Arrowroot Powder
½ tsp Sea Salt	¼ tsp Oregano	

Combine all ingredients.

Tip The arrowroot in this recipe will help thicken the seasoning when added to any meat, much like store-bought spice packs. If you don't care about it being thick, omitting this ingredient will not affect the flavor.

This recipe is Vegan

SWEET CHILI SAUCE

½ cup Coconut Vinegar	2 Tbsp Fish Sauce	1 ½ Tbsp Arrowroot Powder +
⅓ cup Honey	3 cloves Garlic	2 Tbsp Water (= a slurry)
¼ cup Water	2 Red Chili Peppers	

Remove the stems and most of the seeds from the red chili peppers. We like to combine all ingredients except the arrowroot in a blender and blend until the peppers are mostly chopped. Pour these ingredients into a saucepan and bring to a boil. Next, turn the heat down to medium (~4) and cook for about 10 minutes, or until the sauce has reduced by half.

Once reduced, turn the heat down to low and add the slurry. Continue to stir until the right consistency is reached. This will not take long, so watch it carefully.

This recipe is Pescatarian

BALSAMIC GLAZE

1 cup Balsamic Vinegar	3 Tbsp Honey	1 Tbsp Coconut Aminos

Combine all ingredients in a saucepan and bring to a boil. Once boiling, reduce the heat to low and simmer, stirring occasionally, until the glaze is thick and syrupy, about 20 minutes. Remove from heat and let cool.

This recipe is Vegan

REFRIGERATOR DILL PICKLES

10-15 Salad Cucumbers

24 sprigs Fresh Dill

8 cloves Garlic

8 cups Water

2 cups Coconut Vinegar

⅓ cup Fine Sea Salt

6 Tbsp Minced Onion

2 tsp Garlic Powder

2 tsp Honey

1 tsp Ground Mustard

4 Ball Mason Jars

Optional: 24 Carrot Slices

Optional: 40 Black
Peppercorns

Optional: 4 Fresh Serrano
Chili Peppers
(with seeds)

Cut the cucumbers in half lengthwise and place 4–5 cucumber halves, 8 sprigs of fresh dill, 6 carrot slices, 2 garlic cloves, 10 black peppercorns and 1 serrano chili (cut in half) in each jar. Set aside for later.

In a medium saucepan, bring the minced onion, garlic powder, coconut crystals, mustard, water, vinegar, and sea salt to a boil and boil, until the sea salt is completely dissolved.

Once the sea salt is dissolved (which won't take long), pour the hot liquids over the cucumbers and fill until they are covered. Make sure there is an even amount of onion in each. Screw the lids shut, mark the date, and let sit on the counter for 3 days, shaking randomly when you think about it.

After 3 days of the pickles sitting out on the counter, refrigerate overnight. The next day, they're ready to eat! And they stay fresh for about a month!

Tip The carrots, peppercorns, and serrano chilies are all optional, but we like to use them. They give dimension to the pickles and taste great as well!

Tip Muy Importante! You can buy salad pickles from a regular grocery store and not worry about the wax issue for this recipe. I bought them and they worked perfectly. Just in case you don't have those fancy canning pickles, no worries!

This recipe is Vegan

DON AYALA'S SOFRITO

2 cups Fresh Garlic	1 cup Green Bell Peppers	1 cup Sweet Cubanelle Peppers
2 cups Culantro Leaves	3 cups Vidalia Onions	1 cup Olive Oil

Place all ingredients in a food processor and blend until finely minced.

Tip This recipe makes a lot, but we use it for many recipes and it can easily be frozen. We like to freeze it in ice cube trays for individual servings!

Tip If you don't have access to culantro, you can use cilantro.

This recipe is Vegan

RISE AND SHINE

Blueberry Muffins • Herbes De Provence Eggs • Sweet Potato Home Fries
Grits • Pastelón • Pancakes • Meaty Egg Scramble • Fried Green Tomatoes
Sweet Plantain Omelets • Savory Sweet Potato Hash Browns • Waffles
Fluffy Paleo Bread • Cilantro Apple Jam • Egg BLT With Mayonnaise
Dill Shrimp Salad • Breakfast Casserole • Biscuits And Sausage Gravy
Vietnamese Stir-Fry • Bird's Nest Breakfast • Cranberry Tangerine Breakfast Muffins

BLUEBERRY MUFFINS

⅓ cup Almond Flour	¼ tsp Baking Powder	1 Tbsp Vanilla Extract
2 Tbsp Coconut Flour	3 Eggs	¾ cup Blueberries
2 Tbsp Arrowroot Powder	3 ½ Tbsp Honey	*Optional:* Almond Slices
⅛ tsp Sea Salt	2 ½ Tbsp Applesauce	Paper Liners or
	2 Tbsp Coconut Oil	Coconut Oil

Preheat the oven to 350 degrees Fahrenheit.

In a bowl, combine the almond flour, coconut flour, arrowroot powder, and baking powder. Mix until incorporated.

In a blender, combine the eggs, honey, applesauce, sea salt, coconut oil, and vanilla.

Add the wet to the dry (we use a whisk to break up any clumps), then fold in the blueberries.

Grease a set of muffin tins with coconut oil or line each with a paper liner. Fill each tin (6 total) ½ of the way full (unless you like really big, heavy muffins; they go a full ¾).

We sometimes like to top ours with some sliced almonds or something a little sweet. If you do too, in a separate bowl, combine:

- 1 Tbsp Shredded Unsweetened Coconut Flakes
- 1 Tbsp Coconut Crystals
- 1 tsp Cinnamon
- 1 tsp Nutmeg

Sprinkle this mixture on top of the muffins before they go into the oven.

They should be in the oven for 20–25 minutes. In our oven, it's a little closer to 25 minutes—just until a toothpick comes out clean.

Makes 6

This recipe is Vegetarian

HERBES DE PROVENCE EGGS

4 Hard-Boiled Eggs

2 strips Bacon

1 Tomato

3 Mushrooms

3 Asparagus Spears

2 Green Onions

2 cloves Garlic

1 tsp Herbes de Provence

½ Tbsp Olive Oil

Sea Salt and Black Pepper (to taste)

Dice all of the vegetables, discarding the tomato seeds, mushroom stems, and asparagus and green onion bottoms. Mince the garlic and chop the eggs.

Heat the oil over medium-high heat and add the asparagus, bacon, and mushrooms. Sauté for 2–3 minutes. Then add the remaining ingredients and sauté until tender and the eggs are warmed through. Season with sea salt and black pepper and serve.

Serves 2 to 4

This recipe can easily be made Vegetarian; just omit the bacon

SWEET POTATO HOME FRIES

2 Sweet Potatoes

2 tsp Herbes de Provence

2 Tbsp Olive Oil

Sea Salt and Black Pepper
(to taste)

Optional: 2 tsp Sriracha
(Thai hot sauce—we love
this)

Peel and dice the sweet potatoes into ½"
squares. Toss the sweet potatoes with the
herbes de Provence, sea salt, black pepper,
and Sriracha (which is *so* good if you
haven't tried it).

Heat the oil in a pan over medium-high
heat. Add the sweet potatoes, cover, and
cook for 5 minutes. You'll want to shake
or stir the pan, so the sweet potatoes don't
burn on one side.

Tip If you like spicy food, add a couple
teaspoons of Sriracha, which is an addic-
tive Thai hot sauce. Delicious!

Serves 2 to 4

This recipe is Vegan

GRITS

3 cups Grated Cauliflower	⅓ cup Almond Flour	½ cup Coconut Milk
2 Tbsp Arrowroot Powder	1 cup Chicken Stock	Sea Salt and Black Pepper (to taste)

Combine all ingredients in a saucepan. Heat the grits over high heat until they start to boil. Watch them, as this happens quickly. Then turn the heat down to low (~2), cover, and cook for 20 minutes, making sure to stir them frequently.

Uncover and cook for another 5-10 minutes on low heat.

Tip You'll want to put the cauliflower in the food processor so it is grated down to the consistency of grits.

Tip These grits are also great for dinner with our Jambalaya! (see page 115)

Serves 2 to 4

This recipe can easily be made Vegan; just swap the chicken stock with vegetable stock

PASTELÓN

1 lb Ground Beef

1 Tbsp Adobo Seasoning
(see page 14)

3 Black Plantains

2 Tbsp Olive Oil

3 cloves Garlic

3 Bay Leaves

4 Tbsp Ayala's Sofrito
(see page 20)

1 ½ tsp Culantro y Achiote
Seasoning (see page 16)

8 oz Tomato Sauce

8 oz Water

½ tsp Black Pepper

½ tsp Sea Salt

½ tsp Oregano

6 Eggs

Preheat the oven to 350 degrees Fahrenheit. Grease an 8" x 8" glass baking dish and set aside.

Heat the oil over medium-high heat (~7) in a medium-sized saucepan. Mince the garlic and add to the pan. Then add Ayala's Sofrito. You'll want to move it around quite a bit so it doesn't burn. Once it is sizzling, then add the meat and Adobo Seasoning.

Break up the meat and incorporate with Ayala's Sofrito and the garlic. Once you have smaller chunks, add the tomato sauce, water, bay leaves, Culantro y Achiote Seasoning black pepper, sea salt, and oregano. Stir together, cover, and cook for about 15 minutes (or until meat is no longer pink), stirring occasionally.

While the meat is cooking, whip the eggs and set aside.

Remove the outer peel from the plantains and cut lengthwise into long, ⅛" strips.

Layer the ingredients in this order: some plantain, then a little egg, then the meat mixture. Layer the ingredients until there are no additional ingredients and bake uncovered for 30 minutes.

Tip The plantains need to be black. Not green, not yellow, but black. If they are not black, this recipe will not turn out. If you have green plantains, place them somewhere dark and let them turn black.

Serves 4 to 6

PANCAKES

2 Large Eggs

⅓ cup Maple Syrup

1 Tbsp Vanilla Extract

¼ cup Water

2 Tbsp Coconut Oil

½ tsp Sea Salt

¼ cup Golden Flaxseed Meal

1 ¼ cups Almond Flour

½ tsp Baking Powder

1 Tbsp Arrowroot Powder

Coconut Oil

Combine the eggs, maple syrup, vanilla extract, water, coconut oil (liquefied), and sea salt and mix until incorporated. In a separate bowl, mix the golden flaxseed meal, almond flour, baking powder, and arrowroot powder until combined. Or if you are lazy, like me in the mornings, just put all of the ingredients in a blender and go to town. Heat a skillet over medium-low (on my oven, ~4), *then* add a tablespoon of coconut oil.

Make smaller pancakes; the larger you make these, the harder they will be to flip. It only takes a couple of minutes on each side—just make sure that they are a golden brown on each side and you're ready to eat!

They already have maple syrup in them, so they are nice and sweet! We like to top ours with fresh blueberries or other fruits.

Tip We heat a tablespoon of coconut oil for every set of pancakes we make. It makes them a little crispy on the edges and we like that.

Makes 8 to 12

This recipe is Vegetarian

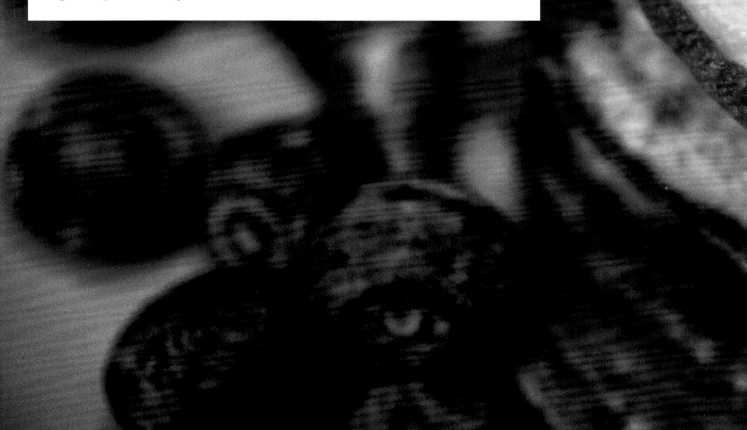

MEATY EGG SCRAMBLE

½ cup Hot Italian Sausage	4 Eggs	1 Tbsp Olive Oil
8 Large Shrimp	¼ Yellow Onion	½ tsp Creole Seasoning
2 Bacon Strips	1 Green Onion	Sea Salt and Black Pepper (to taste)

Dice all ingredients, removing the white part of the green onion.

Heat the olive oil over medium-high heat. Add the sausage and bacon and cook for one minute. Then add the shrimp and yellow onion and season with sea salt, black pepper and Creole seasoning.

Cook until the shrimp starts to turn pink. Then add the eggs and green onions and stir, cooking until the eggs are set and no longer runny.

Serves 2 to 4

FRIED GREEN TOMATOES

3-4 Green Tomatoes	¾ tsp Adobo Seasoning (see page 14)	2 Tbsp Olive Oil
¼ cup Almond Flour	¼ tsp Onion Powder	Rémoulade Sauce (see page 49)
1 Egg	¼ tsp Cayenne Powder	Diced Red Tomatoes
2 Tbsp Coconut Milk	4 Tbsp Walnut Oil	Cilantro or Parsley

Turn the oven to broil (500 degrees Fahrenheit, with heat from the top).

Slice the tomatoes into about ¼" slices.

In one bowl, combine the egg and coconut milk. In another bowl, combine the almond flour, Adobo Seasoning, onion powder, and cayenne powder.

Dip the tomato slices in the egg mixture, then dredge them in the almond flour mixture.

Put the slices onto a greased or parchment-lined baking sheet. Combine the oils and drizzle over the tomatoes.

Broil on the middle rack for 6–7 minutes or until browned, then flip and bake for another 5–6 minutes or until browned.

You can panfry these as well if you prefer. Heat 3–4 tablespoons oil in a pan over medium-high heat and cook for 3–4 minutes on each side. Garnish with diced red tomatoes, our Rémoulade Sauce, and chopped cilantro or parsley.

Makes 12 to 15

This recipe is Vegetarian but can be made Vegan if you omit the egg

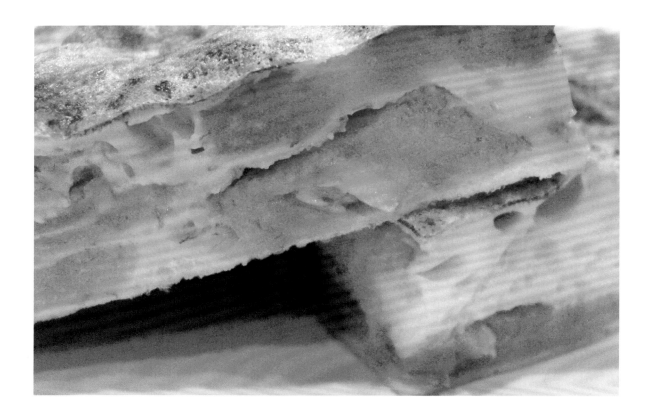

SWEET PLANTAIN OMELETS

6 Eggs

2 Black Plantains

Sea Salt (to taste)

Coconut Oil

Heat a pan over low heat (~3) and add about a teaspoon of coconut oil. (we use coconut oil, but you could just add 1 teaspoon of your favorite oil).

Mix the eggs together and pour half onto the pan. Then slice the plantains in a thin layer on the eggs. Then cover with the rest of the eggs.

Cover the pan with the lid and let cook for 15 minutes.

Once ready, flip onto a plate and cut into 4 pieces.

Tip The plantains need to be black. Not green, not yellow, but black. If they are not black, this recipe will not turn out. If you have green plantains, place them somewhere dark and let them turn black.

Serves 2 to 4

This recipe is Vegetarian

SAVORY SWEET POTATO HASH BROWNS

2 Large Sweet Potatoes

2 Tbsp Extra Virgin Olive
   Oil

½ tsp Garlic

½ tsp Parsley

½ tsp Bell Pepper or Chili
   Pepper

½ tsp Onion Powder

½ tsp Lemon Pepper

½ tsp Sesame Seeds

1 Tbsp Chipotle Pepper
   Sauce

Sea Salt and Black Pepper
   (to taste)

Optional: Chives

Peel the sweet potatoes and then grate them. Toss the gratings with the spices, sea salt, and black pepper. Heat the oil in a skillet over medium to medium-high heat. Add potatoes. Cook until the sweet potatoes are tender, stirring frequently.

Tip If you want the hash browns to be done faster, you can cover the skillet with a lid for a few minutes to steam the potatoes.

Serves 2 to 4

This recipe is Vegan

WAFFLES

1 cup Almond Flour	1 cup Coconut Milk	pinch Sea Salt
½ cup Golden Flaxseed Meal	6 Eggs (separated)	1 Tbsp Coconut Oil
½ cup Coconut Flour	1 Tbsp Vanilla Extract	Coconut Oil
4 Tbsp Maple Syrup	2 tsp Baking Powder	

Combine all ingredients except for the egg whites and sea salt. The flour mix will be fluffy and seem a little dry. This is OK.

In a separate bowl, combine the sea salt and egg whites. Using a hand mixer, beat the egg whites at medium-high speed until stiff peaks appear.

Fold the egg whites into the flour mix. Try not to overmix it; just mix until incorporated. Coat the waffle iron in coconut oil. Use about 1 cup of batter per waffle and cook for about 3 minutes or until golden brown and fluffy.

Tip If you don't have a hand mixer, you can beat the eggs by hand. It will take you quite some time, but it can be done.

Makes 4 to 6

This recipe is Vegetarian

FLUFFY PALEO BREAD

1 ½ cup Arrowroot Powder	4 Egg Whites	4 tsp Baking Powder
1 cup Golden Flaxseed Meal	4 Tbsp Walnut Oil	2 tsp Coconut Vinegar
4 Eggs	2 tsp Sea Salt	Coconut Oil

Preheat the oven to 350 degrees Fahrenheit.

Combine the arrowroot powder, flaxseed meal, and baking powder. In a separate bowl, combine the eggs, egg whites, walnut oil, sea salt, and coconut vinegar.

Next, mix the wet and add to the dry until thoroughly incorporated.

Grease a bread loaf pan with oil. For muffins, bake 20–25 minutes or until a toothpick comes out clean. For the loaf, bake about 30–35 minutes.

Tip Toast this bread and serve with our Cilantro Apple Jam! (see page 36)

Makes 1 loaf

This recipe is Vegetarian

CILANTRO APPLE JAM

3 Gala or Fuji Apples	¼ cup Coconut Crystals	¼ tsp Sea Salt
½ cup Apple Juice	1 Tbsp Ginger	½ Tbsp Arrowroot Powder
Juice of ½ Lemon	½ Tbsp Honey	+ ¼ cup Water (= slurry)
		¼ cup Cilantro

Peel and dice the apples, discarding the core and skins. Add the apples, apple juice, lemon juice, coconut crystals, ginger, honey, and sea salt to a saucepan over medium-high heat (~6) and cook for about 10 minutes, stirring occasionally.

Turn the heat down to medium-low (~3) and simmer, uncovered, for 30–45 minutes or until the apples begin to break down. Next, add the slurry and stir until thickened.

Remove the jam from the heat as soon as it has reached the right consistency. Let it cool for 2 minutes, then add the chopped cilantro. Spoon into a jam jar and refrigerate.

Tip If you like jelly more than jam, puree the mixture before you add the arrowroot and cilantro. Strain it through a sieve, then put it back on the oven and continue with the recipe.

Tip This jam is great with our toasted Fluffy Paleo Bread for breakfast, or as a glaze for pork or chicken!

Tip This recipe is made with fresh Ginger. If you use ground, we can't guarantee the results!

This recipe is Vegan

EGG BLT WITH MAYONNAISE

4 Eggs	Sea Salt and Black Pepper (to taste)	Tomato
6 strips Bacon		Coconut Oil
2 Tbsp Mayonnaise (see page 14)	1 Avocado	*Optional*: Fluffy Paleo Bread (see page 35)
	Lettuce	
	Red Onion	

Heat a pan over medium heat (~5) and add one teaspoon of coconut oil. Once hot, add the eggs in a single layer. Season with salt and black pepper.

While the eggs are cooking, cook the bacon. They will take about the same amount of time. Watch the bacon, flipping occasionally until you reach the desired crispiness.

While the bacon and eggs are cooking, slice the tomatoes, red onion, and avocado.

The eggs should no longer be transparent, but still a little wiggly when you gently shake the pan. We want them to have a gooey center.

Now we create: If using bread, lightly toast it, then spread on a little Mayonnaise, then layer the lettuce, avocado, red onions, bacon, tomatoes, and finally egg. That way, when you break the egg, it runs down the entire sandwich.

Serves 2

DILL SHRIMP SALAD

30 Large Shrimp	4 Tbsp Mayonnaise (see page 14)	¾ cup Sweet Onion
Adobo Seasoning (see page 14)	1 clove Garlic	⅓ cup Cucumber
2 Tbsp Coconut Milk	1 tsp Dill	1 small rib Celery
		Coconut Oil

Peel the raw shrimp and dust them with the Adobo Seasoning, coating lightly. Heat a pan to medium-high heat (~7) and add a teaspoon of coconut oil. Cook the shrimp for about 3-4 minutes on each side or until pink and cooked through. Remove from heat and set aside to let cool.

While the shrimp are cooling, mince the garlic; dice the onion and celery; and peel, de-seed, and dice the cucumber. Put all ingredients in a bowl. Add the coconut milk, Mayonnaise, and dill (reserving a little for garnish).

Next, dice the shrimp and add to the mixture. Chill. Garnish with fresh dill and you're done!

Serves 4 to 6

This recipe is Pescetarian

BREAKFAST CASSEROLE

2 Small Sweet Potatoes	½ Sweet Onion	¼ tsp Sage
3 Tbsp Extra Virgin Olive Oil	1 Tbsp Arrowroot Powder	Sea Salt and Black Pepper (to taste)
1 cup Sausage (we prefer chicken and apple)	4 Eggs	Coconut Oil
	½ cup Coconut Milk	

Grease a glass 8" x 8" baking dish. Preheat the oven to 350 degrees Fahrenheit.

Grate the sweet potatoes and then place them in the bottom of the greased dish.

Heat 2 tablespoons oil over medium-high heat (~7). Dice the onion and sausage and add to the oil. Season with salt and black pepper and cook until the sausage is no longer pink and onions are translucent. Mix in the arrowroot powder.

Layer the sausage and onion on top of the sweet potatoes.

Next, blend the eggs, sage, coconut milk, and ½ teaspoon of both sea salt and black pepper. Pour the egg mixture on top of the sausage and onions.

Bake uncovered for 45 minutes or until a toothpick comes out clean.

Tip This recipe freezes very easily and reheats with a nice flavor. Make it in advance, freeze single serving portions, and reheat it when you're running late!

Serves 4 to 6

This recipe can be made Vegetarian; just omit the sausage

BISCUITS AND SAUSAGE GRAVY

Biscuits:	¼ cup Coconut Flour	6 Egg Whites
½ cup Almond Flour	1 tsp Baking Powder	½ tsp Sea Salt
¼ cup Golden Flaxseed Meal	1 Tbsp Walnut Oil	Coconut Oil

Sausage Gravy:	14 oz Coconut Milk	1 ½ Tbsp Walnut Oil
8 oz Sausage	¼ tsp Fennel Seeds	Sea Salt and Black Pepper (to taste)
1 ½ Tbsp Arrowroot Powder	1 tsp Dried Sage	

Preheat the oven to 400 degrees Fahrenheit.

First, grease 4 large muffin tins with coconut oil. Set aside.

In a large bowl, combine the almond flour, flaxseed meal, coconut flour, and baking powder. Mix thoroughly.

In a blender, combine the walnut oil, sea salt, and egg whites. Blend until frothy, then add the mixture to the dry ingredients. Try not to mix this too much—just enough so that all ingredients are wet.

Fill the pre-oiled muffin tins with the batter (should be about halfway full). Bake in the middle of the oven for about 15 minutes. The tops should be browned a little and the muffins should slide out of the tins easily.

As the biscuits are cooking, we'll make the gravy. So first things first, break up the sausage into chunks. Heat a skillet to medium-high heat (~6) and add the sausage.

Dust the sausage with about half of the arrowroot powder and mix to incorporate,

then add a little oil (again, about half) and mix to incorporate. Do this until the arrowroot powder and oil are gone. Stir the sausage until browned.

While the sausage is browning, combine the coconut milk with the sage and fennel seeds. Add the coconut milk mixture to the sausage, mixing continuously, and then season with sea salt and black pepper to taste.

Tip If you don't have any arrowroot powder, you can use coconut flour as well. You will need a little more and it will take a little longer to set up, but it will work just fine in a pinch.

Tip If you are using pork instead of a leaner meat, you do *not* need as much oil. The walnut will give it a good flavor, but it will get a little oily if you use as much with a fattier sausage.

Serves 4–6

This recipe can be made Vegetarian; just omit the sausage

VIETNAMESE STIR-FRY

1 lb Flank Steak

Adobo Seasoning
   (see page 14)

2 Tbsp Coconut Oil

2 Large Sweet Potatoes

½ cup Green Onions

3 cloves Garlic

1 Shallot

1 Red Chili Pepper

1 tsp Lemongrass

1 ½ Tbsp Lime Juice

1 Tbsp Fish Sauce

Sea Salt and Black Pepper
   (to taste)

½ cup Basil

½ cup Cilantro

To prep, cut the beef into small strips (we aim for ¼" wide by ⅛" thick) and dust with a little Adobo Seasoning. Grate the sweet potatoes (skins on), chop the green onions and shallot, mince the garlic and red chili, and chop the basil and cilantro.

Heat ½ tablespoon of coconut oil over a medium-high heat (~7) pan and sauté the beef for just a minute or two (this recipe is for medium-rare). Set aside.

Reduce the heat to medium (~4) and add the remaining oil if you need it. You may have enough drippings depending on whatever type of meat you are using. You want about a tablespoon or so. Then add the sweet potatoes, green onions, shallot, lemongrass, red chili pepper, garlic, sea salt, and black pepper.

Cover and cook, stirring infrequently, until the potatoes begin to get tender and brown. This will take about 10-15 minutes.

Return the beef to the pan and add the lime juice and fish sauce. Cook until the liquid is soaked up. Toss in the basil and cilantro and serve immediately.

Tip You can use whatever type of beef steak you'd like, but we usually use flank steak or skirt steak for this recipe.

Serves 4

BIRD'S NEST BREAKFAST

4 Poached Eggs

1 lb Grass-Fed Ground
Beef

Adobo Seasoning
Hash Browns
(see page 14)

Savory Sweet Potato
(see page 33)

Optional: Sriracha

Just follow the instructions for our Sweet Potato Hash Browns.

While the hash browns are cooking, season the ground beef with Adobo Seasoning (just a light dusting) and cook until no longer pink.

When the beef is almost done, start making the poached eggs. If you need help with this, go to our blog at www.paleoeffect.com. And again, just follow the recipe.

Now, we layer: savory sweet potato hash browns, beef, then eggs. Like hot sauce? Top it all with some Sriracha!

Serves 4

CRANBERRY TANGERINE
BREAKFAST MUFFINS

⅓ cup Almond Flour	⅛ tsp Sea Salt	¼ cup Honey
2 Tbsp Coconut Flour	3 Eggs	¼ cup Cranberries
2 Tbsp Arrowroot Powder	1 Tbsp Vanilla Extract	¼ cup Tangerines
¼ tsp Baking Powder	2 Tbsp Coconut Oil	*Optional:* Almond Slices
¼ tsp Cinnamon	2 Tbsp Applesauce	Paper Liners or Coconut Oil
¼ tsp Ground Ginger	1 Tbsp Orange Juice	

Preheat the oven to 350 degrees Fahrenheit.

In a bowl, combine the almond flour, coconut flour, arrowroot powder, baking powder, cinnamon, and ginger. Mix until incorporated.

In a blender, combine the eggs, honey, applesauce, orange juice, sea salt, coconut oil, and vanilla.

Add the egg mixture to the flour mixture. We like to use a whisk to break up any clumps. Roughly chop the cranberries (see side tip). De-seed the tangerines and roughly chop as well, then fold in the cranberries and tangerines.

Grease a set of 6 large muffin tins with coconut oil or line each with a paper liner.

Fill each tin ½ of the way full (unless you like really big, heavy muffins; they go a full ¾).

We like to top ours with some sliced almonds.

They should be in the oven for 20–25 minutes—just until a toothpick comes out clean.

Tip We use frozen, de-thawed cranberries for this recipe, so they have already popped open and all we have to do is give them a quick chop. You can use fresh ones but I would chop them finely and sauté them for a second before adding to the batter.

Makes 6

This recipe is Vegetarian

SAUCY

Rémoulade Sauce • Ranch Dip • Honey Mustard Dipping Sauce
Shrimp Sauce • Spicy Honey BBQ Sauce
Sweet Chipotle BBQ Sauce
Teriyaki Sauce • Tomato Sauce with Mushrooms
Pickled Mustard Seed • Avocado Dressing

RÉMOULADE SAUCE

¼ cup Mayonnaise
(see page 14)

1 Tbsp Sweet Chili Sauce
(see page 18)

1 Tbsp Dijon Mustard

½ tsp Sea Salt

¼ tsp Creole Seasoning

Optional: pinch Saffron

Combine all ingredients.

This recipe is Vegetarian

Tip Serve alongside our Crab Cakes!
(see page 57)

RANCH DIP

¼ cup Mayonnaise
(see page 14)

½ tsp Dill

¼ tsp Chives

½ tsp Garlic Powder

¼ tsp Onion Powder

1 Tbsp Lemon Juice

pinch Sea Salt

pinch Black Pepper

Combine all ingredients.

This recipe is Vegetarian

HONEY MUSTARD DIPPING SAUCE

½ cup Mayonnaise
(see page 14)

2 tsp Ground Mustard

½ tsp Garlic Powder

1 Tbsp Coconut Vinegar

2 Tbsp Honey

pinch Sea Salt

pinch Black Pepper

Combine all ingredients in a blender.

This recipe is Vegetarian

Tip Kids love this with our "Breaded"
Chicken Nuggets! (see page 148)

SHRIMP SAUCE

¼ cup Mayonnaise (see page 14)

3 Tbsp Coconut Milk

2 Tbsp Grape-Seed Oil

¾ tsp Paprika

½ tsp Garlic Powder

1 ¼ tsp Ketchup

¼ tsp Coconut Vinegar

pinch Sea Salt

Blend all ingredients until well incorporated.

This recipe is Vegetarian

SPICY HONEY BBQ SAUCE

¼ cup Ketchup

3 Tbsp Honey

1 ½ Tbsp Coconut Aminos

1 Tbsp Coconut Vinegar

2 tsp Onion Powder

1 tsp Chili Powder

1 tsp Garlic Powder

½ tsp Sea Salt

¼ cup Olive Oil

6-8 Dried Arbol Chili Peppers

Blend all ingredients in a blender until smooth. Letting this sit overnight will increase the intensity of the peppers— something to keep in mind if you are making this in advance.

This recipe is Vegan

SWEET CHIPOTLE BBQ SAUCE

1 ½ Tbsp Balsamic Glaze (see page 18)

1 tsp Ground Chipotle Pepper

2 Tbsp Ketchup

¼ cup Olive Oil

1 Tbsp Coconut Vinegar

¼ tsp Chili Powder

¼ tsp Cayenne Powder

Combine all ingredients and blend until smooth.

This recipe is Vegan

Tip Serve over our delicious, fall-off-the-bone Pulled Pork! (see page 139)

TERIYAKI SAUCE

½ cup Coconut Aminos	½ tsp Garlic Powder	1 ½ Tbsp Arrowroot Powder
¾ tsp ground Ginger	3 Tbsp Maple Syrup	½ cup Orange Flower Water

In a small saucepan, combine the coconut aminos, ginger, garlic, and maple syrup. Heat over medium-high (~6).

While the coconut aminos mixture is heating up, mix together the orange flower water and arrowroot powder. Slowly add it to the saucepan, mixing as you go. You don't want clumps.

Heat, stirring, until the desired consistency is reached (about 3–4 minutes).

Tip Try this sauce with skirt steak, chicken, shrimp, or salmon!

Tip If you don't have access to orange flower water, you can just use water. It won't taste quite the same, but it will still be delicious!

This recipe is Vegan

TOMATO SAUCE WITH MUSHROOMS

⅓ Sweet Onion	26 oz Diced Tomatoes	¼ cup Parsley
1 Tbsp Duck Fat	¼ cup Water	⅛ tsp Cayenne Powder
4 cloves Garlic	¾ tsp Black Pepper	1 cup White Button Mushrooms
1 tsp Sea Salt	¼ cup Basil Leaves	

Dice the onions, mushrooms, and garlic, but keep them separate. Heat the fat in a medium-sized saucepan over medium-high heat (~7).

Once hot, add the onions and cook for 3-4 minutes until caramelized (you'll want to stir frequently and continue to cook until the onions are a nice light brown). Once the onions are golden, add the garlic and sea salt and continue to cook for one minute or until the garlic is fragrant.

Add the water and tomatoes and bring to a boil. Set the timer for 1 hour, turn the heat down to low (~2), and stir in the remaining ingredients.

Stir occasionally. Serve when the desired consistency is achieved (for us, it's about an hour on low).

Tip You can use any type of fat, whether it be a lard or oil. We like duck fat because it has a unique flavor, but if you don't have access to this, no worries!

Tip This recipe is great for our Spaghetti and Meatballs! (see page 128)

This recipe can easily be made Vegan; just swap the duck fat with olive oil.

PICKLED MUSTARD SEED

1" chunk Ginger	½ cup Water	½ Tbsp Sea Salt
1 clove Garlic	½ cup Coconut Vinegar	⅓ cup Whole Yellow Mustard Seed
	3 Tbsp Honey	

Combine all ingredients in a saucepan and bring to a simmer. You'll want to turn the heat to high, watch it like a hawk, and just as it starts to boil, turn it down to low (~2.5) and let it simmer for 45-50 minutes.

Stir it frequently and watch it every now and again, especially toward the beginning as the heat is equalizing. You'll know it's done when the seeds are plump.

I hear you: "But what happens if they start to dry out?!" No worries, just take a deep breath and add a little water to make sure that they are submerged, and you'll be fine. You probably won't have to worry about it, but just in case, add water.

When ready, remove the ginger and garlic, and bottle. Store this in the refrigerator.

Tip We use this on everything from our Deviled Eggs (see page 56) to our Corned Beef and Cabbage (see page 130)!

This recipe is Vegan

AVOCADO DRESSING

2 Tbsp Mayonnaise
(see page 14)

1 tsp Coconut Vinegar

1 Hass Avocado

1 tsp Dried Onion Flakes

⅛ tsp Dill

⅛ tsp Garlic Powder

1 tsp Lemon Juice

Combine all ingredients.

Tip Serve this with our Southwestern Chicken Wraps! (see page 149)

This recipe is Vegetarian

STARTERS

Deviled Eggs • Crab Cakes • Arañitas • Restaurant-Style Guacamole • Bacon Wraps
Cocktail Meatballs • Shrimp and Whitefish Ceviche • Shrimp Sliders with Ginger Garlic Aioli
Thai Chicken Wings • Tropical Fruit Salsa

DEVILED EGGS

12 Hard-Boiled Eggs

3 Tbsp Mayonnaise
(see page 14)

¾ tsp Dried Minced Onion

3 cloves Garlic

1 ½ tsp Dijon Mustard

½ tsp Dill

1 ½ tsp Coconut Vinegar

Sea Salt and Black Pepper
(to taste)

Smoked Paprika

Cut the hard-boiled eggs in half. Scoop out the yolk into a bowl.

Add the Mayonnaise, minced onion, minced garlic, mustard, dill (reserving a little for garnish), and coconut vinegar. Season to taste with sea salt and black pepper.

Scoop the mixture into an icing bag or just use a spoon to fill the empty egg white halves. Sprinkle with a little smoked paprika and garnish with fresh dill.

Makes 24

This recipe is Vegetarian

CRAB CAKES

10 oz Cooked Jumbo Lump Crab Meat	1 Egg	¼ cup Sweet Onion
1 Green Onion	⅓ cup Breadcrumbs (see page 15)	½ tsp Coconut Aminos
1 Tbsp Cilantro	1 clove Garlic	Sea Salt and Black Pepper
2 Tbsp Mayonnaise (see page 14)	½ Tbsp Stone-Ground Dijon Mustard	Pinch Cayenne Powder
1 tsp Lemon Juice	¼ cup Celery	Coconut Oil

Mince the garlic and finely dice the celery and onion. Combine all ingredients except the coconut oil, taking care not to break apart too much of the crab. We like to mix everything else first, then add the crab.

Take a ⅓ measuring cup and fill it with the mixture. Turn it out into your hand and smash it into a flat, round disk, about ¼" thick. Do this for all of the mixture.

Heat 3–4 tablespoons of coconut oil over medium-high heat (~7). Once hot, add the crab cakes.

Cook on each side for about 2–3 minutes. Be very careful on the flip! They are delicate and need to be flipped carefully or else they will fall apart. Cook another 1–2 minutes, until brown.

Tip Serve with our Rémoulade Sauce! (see page 49)

Makes 5 to 6

This recipe is Pescatarian

ARAÑITAS

| 3 Green Plantains | ¼ cup Olive Oil | Coconut Oil |
| 3 cloves Garlic | Sea Salt | Cilantro |

First, mince the garlic and combine it with the olive oil. Let sit for one hour.

Peel the green plantains. This is much more difficult than a banana and you will want to use a knife to get started. Cut the top and bottom off each plantain, then run a knife down one edge. Get your fingers under the edge and peel. Once you get the peel off, soak each plantain for 30 minutes in a sea salt and cold water bath. Add enough sea salt so that the plantains are floating.

After 30 minutes, remove the plantains from the water, dry slightly with a paper towel, and grate them into shreds. Season the plantain shreds with sea salt, then form handful-sized flattened "pancakes" with the green plantain mixture.

Heat about 2" of coconut oil over medium-high heat (about 350 degrees Fahrenheit) in a large enough pan to fry a few arañitas at the same time. Do a test with a piece of plantain. It should sizzle when dropped into the oil. You will want to drop one layer of arañitas into the pan. Don't overcrowd and don't overlap or else they won't cook properly. Fry until they turn a golden brown, which should be about 4–5 minutes on each side. Once golden, remove from the oil and set on a paper-towel lined plate to drain.

Sprinkle with sea salt and chopped cilantro (if you'd like) and serve warm.

Tip The green plantains *must* be green. Not a little yellow, not brown, and definitely *not* black. Green. Very, very green.

Tip Serve with our Guacamole! (see page 59)

Serves 12 to 15

This recipe is Vegan

RESTAURANT-STYLE GUACAMOLE

4 Hass Avocados	1 cup White Onion	1 Tbsp Olive Oil
Juice of 2 Limes	1 ½ cups Cilantro	Sea Salt (to taste)
1 cup Tomato		

Dice all ingredients and combine.

If you are making this Sunday-style (lazy, like we usually do) in a food processor, start by tossing in the onions, cilantro, and lime juice. Pulse until the onions are almost the size you want. Then scrape them out of the way of the blade a little and add everything else (roughly chopped, of course). Season with sea salt and serve.

Tip Serve this with our Arañitas!

Serves 6 to 8

This recipe is Vegan

BACON WRAPS

½ cup Whole Water Chestnuts

4-5 strips Bacon

Coconut Aminos

Coconut Crystals or Honey

Toothpicks

Preheat the oven to 350 degrees Fahrenheit.

Lay out the bacon on a cutting board. Depending on how much bacon you like, cut the bacon into equal strips. We use thick-cut bacon, which will give you more bang for your buck. Cut it in half lengthwise, then cut the 2 strips into 3 equal pieces (so you will have 6 pieces per bacon strip).

Next, dip a water chestnut in the coconut aminos. If you are using honey, you can either dip the water chestnut in it or mix it into the coconut aminos.
If you are using coconut crystals, pour some into a bowl. Dip the bacon in the coconut aminos, then roll the water chestnut into the coconut crystals. Wrap the water chestnut in bacon and secure the meat with a toothpick.

So it goes: water chestnut > coconut aminos > coconut crystals > bacon > toothpick > baking sheet.

Spread out on a baking sheet and bake for about 15 minutes or until bacon is sizzling and cooked.

Makes 25 to 30

COCKTAIL MEATBALLS

Sauce:

⅓ cup Ketchup

¼ cup Sweet Chili
Sauce (see
page 18)

2 Tbsp Coconut
Aminos

2 Tbsp Honey

1 clove Garlic

¼ cup Sweet
Onion

Sea Salt and
Black Pepper
(to taste)

Meatballs:

1 lb Lean Grass-Fed
Ground Beef

½ cup Breadcrumbs
(see page 15)

1 Egg

2 Tbsp Water

1 Tbsp Sweet
Chili Sauce
(see page 18)

3 Tbsp Sweet
Onion

Preheat the oven to 350 degrees Fahrenheit. Grease a baking sheet.

In a bowl, mix the Breadcrumbs with the egg, water, Sweet Chili Sauce, and minced yellow onion. Then add the beef and mix until thoroughly incorporated.

Roll into about 2" balls and place on the greased baking sheet. Bake for 22–25 minutes total, turning once around the 10-minute mark.

While the meatballs are baking, let's make the sauce. Combine the ketchup, Sweet Chili Sauce, coconut aminos, honey, minced garlic, and minced onion in a saucepan. Season the sauce with sea salt and black pepper, to taste.

Once the meatballs are done baking, add them to the sauce and heat over medium-high heat until the sauce is hot and the onions look translucent. You can turn them on low until ready to serve, or put them in a slow cooker and leave them there for guests to graze on.

Makes 20 to 22

SHRIMP AND WHITEFISH CEVICHE

9 Jumbo Shrimp	1 Red Chili Pepper	Juice of 2 Limes
3 (6 oz) Whitefish (such as Grouper or Cod)	½ Red Onion	½ cup Pineapple Juice
1 Tomato	1 Tbsp Fresh Ginger	½ cup Cilantro
	Juice of 1 Lemon	

Peel, de-vein, and de-tail the shrimp. Dice the shrimp and fish and place them in a bowl.

Dice the tomato (we remove the seeds), onion, chili pepper, (we remove the seeds and stems) and cilantro. Mince the ginger. Combine all ingredients with the fish and shrimp.

Cover and refrigerate until the fish is cooked through by the acidity of the citrus juices. You'll want to stir it all up every 30 minutes or so to make sure that the fish gets exposed to the juices. This usually takes a couple of hours.

Tip Serve this with our Arañitas or Tostones! (see page 58) or www.paleoeffect.com!

Serves 2 to 4

This recipe is Pescatarian

SHRIMP SLIDERS
WITH GINGER GARLIC AIOLI

12 oz Shrimp	1 Small Carrot	*Ginger Garlic Aioli:*
1 Shallot	1 tsp Lemongrass	¼ cup Mayonnaise
1 Green Onion	1 tsp Honey	(see page 14)
1 Egg	½ tsp Sea Salt	¼ tsp Garlic
⅓ cup Breadcrumbs	⅛ tsp White Pepper	¼ tsp Ginger
(see page 15)	Coconut Oil	
1 clove Garlic	Cilantro	
1 Tbsp Coconut Aminos	Baby Spinach	

Combine the shallot, green onion (sans the white part), egg, Breadcrumbs, garlic clove, coconut aminos, carrot, lemongrass, honey, sea salt, and white pepper in a food processor and blend until incorporated. You can do this by hand, but you will want to mince the carrots, garlic, shallot, and green onion. Then add in the shrimp and process it until there are only a few large chunks left. We still want it to have chunks of shrimp, but it needs to stick together as well.

Take about ¼ cup of the mixture and form a patty in the palm of your hand. Do this until the mixture is used.

Heat about 2 tablespoons of coconut oil in a pan over medium heat (~5). Add one layer of shrimp sliders, cover, and cook for about 3–4 minutes on each side, or until browned. We like to uncover ours for the last couple of minutes; they seem to stick together better that way.

While these are cooking, prepare your Mayonnaise and add the garlic and ginger after the final step.

Drain the shrimp burgers on paper towels and serve: baby spinach, then shrimp sliders, then Ginger Garlic Aioli, then cilantro! If you are feeling very ambitious, lightly fry the spinach first!

Makes 6 to 8

This recipe is Pescatarian

THAI CHICKEN WINGS

¼ cup Honey

3 Tbsp Coconut Aminos

2 Tbsp Fish Sauce

Juice of ½ Lime

¼ cup Sweet Chili Sauce (see page 18)

½ tsp Sesame Oil

Coconut Oil (if frying)

Free-Range Chicken Wings

Put all ingredients in a blender and blend until all ingredients are incorporated (about a minute).

For Grilling: We suggest medium-high heat, for about 5–7 minutes on each side.

For Oven Roasting: Cover the wings with sauce. You can use a brush after you put them on a baking sheet, or you can pour some in the bowl and toss to coat. Spread them out on an ungreased baking sheet or, better yet, a grill pan. Either way, make sure that the pan you use has a lip to catch the juices. Make sure that the oven is preheated to 300 degrees Fahrenheit. Bake your chicken wings for about an hour and a half. I'd check them at an hour and fifteen and go from there.

When they are done, toss them in a bowl with more of our Thai BBQ sauce if you like them extra saucy.

For Frying: We suggest medium-high heat (~7), and I would use coconut oil and sesame oil. For every 1 tablespoon of coconut oil, add ¼ teaspoon sesame oil. Cook about 4–5 minutes on each side. Make sure that your wings are dry before they go in the oil, too.

Or, you could fry the skin for just a second (on high heat) and then follow our oven recipe. That way, the skin would be really crispy, but it wouldn't be completely fried.

Makes 12–16

TROPICAL FRUIT SALSA

½ cup Pineapple	¼ cup Mango	½ cup Cilantro
¾ cup Cantaloupe Melon	¼ cup Red Onion	¼ tsp Sea Salt
⅓ cup Honeydew Melon	2 Dried Arbol Chili Peppers	1 Tbsp Lime Juice

Dice the fruit and vegetables. Remove the stems from the arbol chili peppers and finely mince. Combine with all additional ingredients. This can be made in advance, but by only a day or so, or the melons get squishy—and nobody likes squishy melons!

Tip This salsa is great with our Coconut-Crusted Cod! (see page 157)

This recipe is Vegan

SOUPS

Ginger Carrot Soup • Strawberry Soup • Thai Cilantro Soup with Scallops
Seafood Gumbo • Egg Drop Soup • Chicken Soup
Coconut-Curried Butternut Squash Soup • Tomato Bisque
Southwestern Red Pepper Soup • Chipotle Bison Chili

GINGER CARROT SOUP

1 lb Carrots	1 Tbsp Celery	1 tsp Madras Yellow Curry Powder
1 Tbsp Coconut Oil	1 cup Coconut Milk	
1 Sweet Onion	1 cup Chicken Stock	1 tsp White Pepper
2 cloves Garlic	1 cup Beef Stock	1 tsp Sea Salt
2 Tbsp Ginger	1 Tbsp Maple Syrup	

Heat the coconut oil over medium-high heat (~7). Dice the onion and add to the oil. Sauté until the onion is almost translucent, then add the garlic and ginger and stir until fragrant (about a minute).

Then add all remaining ingredients. Bring to a boil, then reduce the heat to low (~3), cover, and cook for 30 minutes, stirring occasionally.

After 30 minutes, put the soup in a blender or food processor and blend until smooth. Serve with green onions for garnish.

Serves 4

This recipe can easily be made Vegan; just swap the chicken and beef stocks with vegetable stock

STRAWBERRY SOUP

| 2 cups Strawberries | 1 cup Coconut Milk | 5 Mint Leaves |
| 1 cup Orange Juice | 1 Vanilla Bean | |

Hull and chop the strawberries, discarding the stems. Scrape the insides of the vanilla bean out with the back of a knife. Combine all ingredients in a food processor or blender and puree. Serve chilled and garnish with strawberries.

Tip This particular soup is sweet and best served cold, like a gazpacho.

Serves 2 to 4

This recipe is Vegan

THAI CILANTRO SOUP WITH SCALLOPS

⅓ Diced Yellow Onion	½ cup Broccoli Florets	2 Tbsp Lime Juice
⅓ Diced Red Bell Pepper	1 tsp Garlic	4 Dried Arbol Chili Peppers
½ cup Sliced Mushrooms	1 tsp Ginger	Sea Salt and White Pepper (to taste)
2 cups Chicken Stock	2 Tbsp Coconut Oil	Scallops
1 cup Coconut Milk	½ cup Cilantro	Coconut Oil

To prep, dice the onions and red peppers. Slice the mushrooms. Mince the ginger and garlic.

In a saucepan, heat the oil over medium-high heat (~7) and sauté the onions. When almost translucent, add the bell peppers, garlic, and ginger. Cook about 2 minutes, then add the mushrooms. Cook another minute or two, then add the coconut milk, stock, and arbol chili peppers (remove the stems).

Bring the mix to a boil, then reduce the heat to medium (~4). Add the broccoli and simmer until the broccoli is bright green. Add the lime juice, chopped cilantro, sea salt, and white pepper to taste.

While the soup is simmering, cook the scallops. Heat one teaspoon of coconut oil over medium heat (~5). Set down one layer of scallops, cover, and cook for about 4 minutes or until the scallops bounce back to the touch (push down in the middle of the scallop; if it is ready, it will be just slightly firm and bounce back to the touch).

Tip You can use any type of scallops. You can substitute the scallops with shrimp or even chicken, or leave them out altogether for a completely vegan dish!

Serves 4

This recipe can easily be made Vegan; just omit the scallops

SEAFOOD GUMBO

1 lb Seafood (we use Octopus, Calamari, Shrimp, and Mussels)	4 cloves Garlic	3 Bay Leaves
	3 Tbsp Walnut Oil	¼ cup Shrimp Stock
1 Sweet Yellow Onion	3 Tbsp Olive Oil	¾ cup Clam Juice
1 cup Celery	¼ cup + 1 Tbsp Arrowroot Powder	1 cup Beef Stock
1 Red Pepper		2 cups Water
⅔ cup Diced Okra	1 ½ tsp Old Bay	¼ tsp White Pepper
	5 Dried Arbol Chili Peppers	Sea Salt (to taste)

Cut the ends from the okra and slice into ¼" medallions. Set aside. Then mince the garlic and set it aside too. Then chop and dice all vegetables and set them aside as well.

Heat the oils in a saucepan over medium-high heat. The oils will get very thin and liquid-esque when ready. Add the ¼ cup arrowroot powder to make a roux. Stir the roux and keep stirring for about 5 minutes.

Then add the okra. Mix it around with the roux until browned. Then add the chopped vegetables and cook, stirring, about 5 minutes. The roux will turn brown. This is supposed to happen, so no worries. Add the garlic and sauté until fragrant (about a minute).

After the onions start to become translucent, add the liquids, spices, and seafood and simmer on low heat (~3) for *at least*

30 minutes, uncovered. I suggest an hour. This soup is better if you give it time for the flavors to gel. Be sure to wait at least 30 minutes before seasoning with sea salt. The seafood will release some of its natural sea salt flavors, and you don't want to oversalt. So do the seasoning toward the end.

The flavor of the seafood will be lighter the less you cook it. In an hour, the soup will have a nice, even seafood flavor, and everything will be tender and delicious.

Tip We've been told that a gumbo just isn't a gumbo without okra, but if you aren't in the South and you don't like it or want to use it, this recipe will be just as good without.

Serves 4

This recipe can be made Pescatarian; just swap the beef stock with vegetable stock

EGG DROP SOUP

3 cups Chicken Stock	2 Eggs	pinch White Pepper
1 cup Beef Stock	1 ½ Tbsp Arrowroot Powder + 1 Tbsp Water (= slurry)	pinch Ground Ginger
1 tsp Sea Salt		1 Tbsp Green Onions

Combine the chicken and beef stocks, sea salt, ground ginger, and white pepper and bring to a boil. Once boiling, reduce to medium-high (~6) to prevent boiling over in the next step. We want the soup to be simmering.

In a bowl, lightly beat the eggs until incorporated.

This next step is open to a little interpretation on your part. If you like your soup to have thin ribbons of egg, then with a fork, swirl in a little egg at a time into the hot stock. If you like bigger chunks, then drop in more egg at a time. I like to swirl mine.

Once you have enough of the desired egg in your soup, in a separate cup or bowl, take the arrowroot and combine with a tablespoon of water, or more if you need, until the arrowroot is dissolved. Then add the liquid (called a slurry) to the hot soup. Stir it around until you reach the desired thickness, then garnish with chopped green onions and serve immediately.

Serves 4

This recipe can easily be made Vegetarian; just swap the chicken and beef stocks with vegetable stock

CHICKEN SOUP

12 cups Water	4 Carrots	1 ½ Whole Black Peppercorns
5 Chicken Thighs (with bone)	4 ribs Celery	1 Bay Leaf
	6 Mushrooms	6 sprigs Parsley
1 Tbsp Adobo Seasoning (see page 14)	1 Yellow Onion	3 sprigs Thyme
	2 cloves Garlic	2 tsp Sea Salt

In a large pot, combine the water, chicken thighs, 2 coarsely chopped carrots, 2 coarsely chopped celery ribs, a peeled and quartered onion, smashed garlic cloves, and herbs and bring them to a boil. Cover the stockpot, but leave a little room for steam to release. Simmer for 30 minutes.

Take the chicken out of the pot and remove the skin. You can discard that part. Once cool enough, pull the meat from the bones. Cut the chicken into ½" chunks and set aside for later. Throw the bones back into the stockpot and simmer on medium-low heat (~4) for about 20 minutes. Then strain the broth, discarding the chunks, and put the liquid back into the stockpot. Bring it to a boil, then simmer until reduced, about 30 minutes.

Peel and slice the carrots. Slice the celery and mushrooms. Add them to the strained broth, cover, and simmer until tender, about 10 minutes. Serve and enjoy!

Serves 4 to 6

COCONUT-CURRIED
BUTTERNUT SQUASH SOUP

1 Medium Butternut Squash	1 clove Garlic	1 ½ tsp Sea Salt
14 oz Coconut Milk	½ Tbsp Ginger	Fresh Chopped Cilantro
2 cups Vegetable Stock	1 Tbsp Arrowroot Powder	Adobo Seasoning (see page 14)
2 Tbsp Coconut Oil	3 tsp Red Curry Paste	Large Shrimp
1 Small Sweet Onion	2 tsp Coconut Crystals	Coconut Oil

Heat the coconut oil in a large pot over medium-high heat. Dice the onion, garlic, and ginger. Add the onion to the oil and cook, stirring occasionally, until the onion is almost translucent. Once the onion is ready, add the ginger and garlic and cook until fragrant, about one minute.

Stir the curry paste, coconut crystals, arrowroot powder, and sea salt into the onion mixture and cook for another minute.

To the pot, add the peeled and cubed butternut squash, coconut milk, and stock and turn the heat to high. Bring to a boil, then reduce the heat to low (~3) and simmer for 20–25 minutes.

Peel and de-vein the shrimp. Dust the shrimp with Adobo Seasoning and heat a pan to medium-high heat (~7). Add one teaspoon of coconut oil and cook the shrimp for 5–7 minutes, turning once, or until the shrimp are pink and opaque all the way through.

While the shrimp are cooking, blend the squash soup mixture in a blender or food processor and blend until smooth and creamy.

Top the soup with shrimp and cilantro or shaved coconut and serve immediately.

Serves 4

This recipe can easily be made Vegan; just omit the shrimp

TOMATO BISQUE

1 Tbsp Walnut Oil

2 strips Bacon

1 Small Sweet Onion

1 Carrot

1 stalk Celery

4 cloves Garlic

3 Tbsp Arrowroot
    Powder

4 cups Chicken Stock

26 oz Strained
    Tomatoes

¼ cup Fresh Parsley

4 sprigs Thyme

1 sprig Rosemary

1 Bay Leaf

Sea Salt and Black
    Pepper (to taste)

Heat a pan to medium-high heat (~7). Dice and cook the bacon. When crispy, remove the bacon bits from the grease and set aside for later (either use as a garnish for the soup or on a sandwich).

Chop the onion, carrot, celery, and garlic and add them to the bacon fat. Stir to coat all of the vegetables and then cover and cook for 8 minutes, stirring occasionally.

When soft, stir in the arrowroot powder. If you choose not to use this, the recipe will still taste great, but it just won't have that great bisque texture (it won't be as thick).

Once coated, pour in the walnut oil, stock, parsley, thyme, rosemary, bay leaf, and the tomatoes and bring to

a boil. Reduce the heat to medium-low (~3) and cook, uncovered, for 30 minutes, stirring occasionally.

Pull out the bay leaf and the stems from the rosemary and parsley. Put everything else in a blender or food processor and blend until smooth.

You can keep this in the oven on low to keep it warm. It really is best when piping hot!

Tip Toast some of our Fluffy Paleo Bread with garlic and herbs on the side! (see page 35)

Serves 4

This recipe can easily be made Vegan; just swap the chicken stock with vegetable stock and omit the bacon

SOUTHWESTERN RED PEPPER SOUP

2 Red Peppers

½ Red Onion

⅓ cup Mushrooms

1 clove Garlic

1 Sweet Potato

1 Carrot

2 cups Chicken Stock

1 cup Beef Stock

½ Tbsp Coconut
    Vinegar

½ tsp Cumin

1 Tbsp Cilantro

4 strips Bacon

2 Green Onions

Sea Salt and Black
    Pepper (to taste)

Optional: 1 tsp Red
    Pepper Flakes

Let's first process the vegetables. You want to remove the seeds, stems, and veins from the red peppers—unless you want it hot; then leave some veins and seeds in. Peel the sweet potato and carrot, then roughly chop all the red peppers, onion, mushrooms, garlic clove, sweet potato and carrot.

Heat the oil over medium-high heat and add the vegetables. You want to stir them around until the onions are slightly caramelized (i.e., browned).

Once the onions are caramelized, then add the chicken and beef stocks, coconut vinegar, and cumin. Bring to a boil, then simmer for 30–45 minutes, or until all vegetables are *very* soft. You want to barely poke them with a fork and they should fall apart. If not, your soup will be lumpy instead of creamy.

Once soft, add the cilantro and blend it until it is creamy and smooth. Then put it back in the pan, season with sea salt and black pepper, and place it on the burner on low until ready to serve.

For the garnish, dice the bacon very finely. I like to almost mince it if I have the time. Over medium-high heat (~7), cook the bacon until it is dark and crispy. Remove it from the heat.

In a bowl, ladle out the soup, add chopped green onions (discarding the white parts), then bacon. I like to drizzle a little of the bacon grease around it to pump up the flavor.

Tip If you don't like bacon, you could do the same process as the bacon, but with chicken. Just dust it with a little Adobo Seasoning (see page 14) and cumin.

Serves 4

This recipe can easily be made Vegan; just swap the chicken and beef stocks with vegetable stock

CHIPOTLE BISON CHILI

2 lbs ground Grass-fed Bison	3 Carrots	1 Tbsp Arrowroot Powder
1 Tbsp Adobo Seasoning (see page 14)	1 Green Pepper	1 Tbsp ground Chipotle Pepper
	½ cup Water	
1 Tbsp Duck Fat	1 cup Beef Stock	1 ½ tsp Cumin
1 Sweet Onion	26 oz Crushed Tomatoes	Sea Salt and Black Pepper (to taste)
3 cloves Garlic	1 Tbsp Chili Powder	10 Basil Leaves

Peel and dice the carrots, onions, garlic, and green pepper, keeping them separated.

Heat the oil in a large stockpot over medium-high heat (~7). Add the carrots and sauté about 2 minutes. Then add the onions. Stir until golden brown (caramelized). Once golden, add the green peppers, garlic, arrowroot powder, chili powder, chipotle pepper, and cumin. Stir until incorporated.

Lightly season the meat with a little Adobo Seasoning. Then add it to the vegetables and stir, cooking until no longer pink. Once cooked, add the tomatoes, water, and beef stock. Stir to incorporate. Season with sea salt and black pepper. Turn down the heat to medium-low (~3).

Technically, the chili is done, but we like to let it simmer on medium-low for a while. You can cover the pot or leave it uncovered, but the longer you let it sit, the more the flavors will mingle. Maybe 10 minutes before serving, add the chopped basil leaves and stir in, reserving some basil for garnish.

Serves 4

GREENS

Apple Fennel Salad • Lemon Vinaigrette • Greek Salad • Cobb Salad • Honey Mustard Salad Dressing
Spinach and Apple Salad • Shrimp and Bacon Salad • French Salad Dressing
Turkey Waldorf Salad • Pesto Salad Dressing • Kelp Noodle Salad • Pomegranate Apple Salad
Sesame Ginger Salad Dressing • Japanese Ginger Salad Dressing
Strawberry and Tomato Red Salad • Sweet Poppy Seed Salad • Ranch Salad Dressing
Curried Chicken Salad • Tuna Salad • Chicken Salad

APPLE FENNEL SALAD

1 Honeycrisp Apple

1 Fennel Bulb

¼ cup Walnuts

Lemon Vinaigrette
(see page 83)

Combine all ingredients for the dressing in a blender and blend until thoroughly incorporated (if you like a thicker dressing, slowly add in more oil while whisking to emulsify the dressing).

Core and slice the apple into ⅛" slices. Then do the exact same thing to the fennel. You will want to cut off the tops, then take the cores out, then thinly slice the rest (or use a food processor and discard the cores).

Toss the apple with the fennel and wal- nut pieces and then toss with the Lemon Vinaigrette dressing until coated to your liking. The recipe for Lemon Vinaigrette makes more than what we usually use for this salad, so just put as much as you'd like on it.

Tip If you are Primal and eat a little dairy, goat cheese is wonderful on this salad.

Serves 2 to 4

This recipe is Vegan

LEMON VINAIGRETTE

¼ cup Red Onion	2 Tbsp Olive Oil	½ tsp Black Pepper
¼ cup Meyer Lemon Juice	2 Tbsp Coconut Vinegar	½ tsp Sea Salt

Blend all ingredients together until smooth. This is not meant to be a thick salad dressing.

Tip We prefer Meyer lemons, as they are sweeter, but if you don't have access to them, regular lemons will taste great too.

This recipe is Vegan

GREEK SALAD

1 head Romaine Lettuce	*Greek Salad Dressing:*	*Paleo Croutons:*
1 Tomato	2 cloves Garlic	2 cups Fluffy Paleo Bread (see page 35)
½ Red Onion	1 Tbsp Oregano	½ tsp Garlic Powder
1 Tbsp Chives	6 Tbsp Olive Oil	½ tsp Onion Powder
½ cup Paleo Croutons	½ Tbsp Olive Juice (or Coconut Vinegar if you don't use brine)	½ tsp Sea Salt
1 English Cucumber	Juice of ½ Lemon	½ tsp Black Pepper
1 Red Pepper	½ tsp Sea Salt	½ tsp Oregano
	½ tsp Black Pepper	2-3 Tbsp Olive Oil

Let's make the croutons first. Preheat the oven to 400 degrees Fahrenheit.

Toss all crouton ingredients in a bowl and coat evenly. Spread out on a baking sheet and bake until golden brown, about 10 minutes.

You will want to watch these, as once they are done, they will quickly go from perfect to burnt.

Now for the salad dressing: blend all salad dressing ingredients until thoroughly incorporated.

Dice or slice the tomato, onion, chives, cucumber, and red pepper. Toss with salad dressing and top with croutons.

Tip When making croutons, it's good for this bread to be stale. We like to make these croutons with whatever we have left over from making sandwiches with our Fluffy Paleo Bread recipe.

Serves 2 to 4

This recipe can easily be made Vegan; just omit the croutons

COBB SALAD

3 Hard-Boiled Eggs

¼ cup dried Cranberries

3 strips Bacon

1 Small Tomato

1 Green Onion

1-2 Tbsp Toasted Almonds

½ Red Onion

1 head Romaine or Butter
Leaf Lettuce

Honey Mustard Salad
Dressing (see below)

Optional: Meat such as
Grilled Chicken

Peel and slice the hardboiled eggs.

Cook the bacon and reserve the grease for our Balsamic Glaze or our French Salad Dressing.

Chop the tomato, the green onion, and the red onion.

Break the lettuce apart and add all ingredients. Toss in dressing and serve.

Tip Need help with the hard-boiled eggs? Visit our blog at www.paleoeffect.com!

Tip If you plan to toast your own almonds, heat a pan over medium-high heat (~7). Then add the sliced almonds, ½ tablespoon of olive oil (or coconut or grape-seed), and 1 teaspoon of honey. Toast until browned.

Serves 2 to 4

This recipe can easily be made Vegetarian; just omit the bacon

HONEY MUSTARD SALAD DRESSING

½ cup Olive Oil

2 Tbsp Coconut Vinegar

2 Tbsp Honey

3 Tbsp Dijon Mustard

¼ tsp Garlic Powder

1 small clove Garlic

1 Tbsp Mayonnaise
(see page 14)

Sea Salt and White Pepper
(to taste)

Blend all ingredients together until smooth and incorporated.

Tip This salad dressing is great over our Cobb Salad!

This recipe is Vegetarian

SPINACH AND APPLE SALAD

Warm Bacon Vinaigrette:	Reserved Bacon Fat	¼ tsp Sea Salt
1 Tbsp Coconut Vinegar	4 strips Bacon	¼ tsp Black Pepper
¼ tsp Dijon Mustard	1 Granny Smith Apple	1 Tbsp Chives
¼ cup Olive Oil	2 handfuls Baby Spinach	¼ cup Pecans
1 Tbsp Honey	2 handfuls Arugula	2 Shallots

Dice and cook the bacon over medium-high heat (~7) until crispy, reserving the bacon fat for the salad dressing.

Chop the apple and shallots into slices, and the chives and pecans into small pieces.

In a separate bowl, mix together the coconut vinegar, Dijon mustard, and bacon fat. Whisk in olive oil until the desired consistency is reached; the more oil you add, the thicker it will become i.e., emulsifying. We don't use too much—about 2 tablespoons.

Toss the spinach, chives, pecans, onion, and bacon with the desired amount of Warm Bacon Vinaigrette.

Tip If you are Primal and eat a little dairy, goat cheese is wonderful on this salad.

Serves 2 to 4

This recipe can easily be made Vegan; just omit the eggs and bacon

SHRIMP AND BACON SALAD

4 servings Large Shrimp

½ Tbsp Adobo Seasoning
(see page 14)

2 Tbsp Olive Oil

1 Small Tomato

1 Avocado

3 strips Bacon

¼ cup sliced Almonds

½ Small Red Onion

1 head Romaine Lettuce

Sea Salt and Black Pepper
(to taste)

French Salad Dressing
(see below)

Dice the tomato, red onion, and avocado and toss them in the French Salad Dressing.

Dice and cook the bacon until crispy. Add it to the dressing and vegetables as well.

Heat 1 tablespoon of bacon fat over medium-high heat (~7), add the almond slices, and toast until lightly browned.

Coat the shrimp in the Adobo Seasoning. You don't need that much, just a light dusting. Cook the shrimp in a little olive oil over medium-high heat until pink and

cooked through. Don't forget to season with sea salt and black pepper as you cook the shrimp.

Toss all remaining ingredients together and serve.

Serves 2 to 4

This recipe can easily be made Vegan; just omit the shrimp and bacon

FRENCH SALAD DRESSING

2 Tbsp Coconut Vinegar

1 Tbsp Coconut Crystals

¼ cup Ketchup

1 small clove Garlic

¼ cup Olive Oil

½ tsp Garlic Powder

½ tsp Smoked Paprika

1 Tbsp Coconut Aminos

Sea Salt and Black Pepper
(to taste)

1 strip Bacon + Fat

Dice and cook the bacon. Combine all ingredients and blend until smooth.

This recipe can easily be made Vegan; just omit the bacon

TURKEY WALDORF SALAD

1 head Romaine Lettuce

1 cup Diced Turkey

⅓ cup Blueberries

1 Sliced Apple

¼ cup Walnut Pieces

¼ cup Celery

¼ cup Dried Cranberries

Waldorf Salad Dressing:

¼ cup Mayonnaise
(see page 14)

1 tsp Dijon Mustard

3 Tbsp Olive Oil

1 tsp Lemon Juice

¼ tsp Sea Salt

¼ tsp Black Pepper

½ Tbsp Fresh Parsley

pinch Dried Tarragon

Combine all dressing ingredients and blend until smooth. Combine all salad ingredients in a bowl, then add the desired amount of dressing and toss until thoroughly coated.

Serves 2 to 4

This recipe can easily be made Vegetarian; just omit the turkey

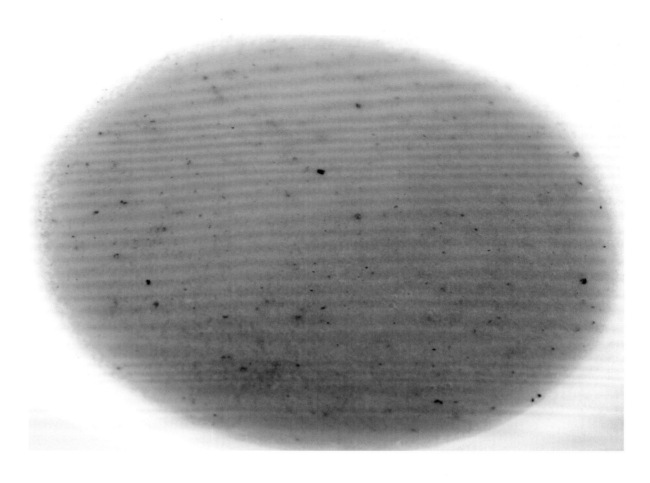

PESTO SALAD DRESSING

½ Tbsp Pine Nuts	1 Tbsp Coconut Vinegar	¼ tsp Sea Salt
1 clove Garlic	½ tsp Lemongrass	¼ tsp Black Pepper
6 Large Basil Leaves	¼ cup Olive Oil	

Combine all ingredients and blend until smooth in consistency.

This recipe is Vegan

Tip See our blog at www.paleoeffect.com for great salad ideas to go with this delicious recipe!

KELP NOODLE SALAD

1 lb package Kelp Noodles

2 Tbsp Coconut Aminos

1 Tbsp Coconut
    Vinegar

1 ½ Tbsp Maple
    Syrup

1 clove Garlic

½ tsp Sesame Oil

1 ½ tsp Ginger

1 Tbsp Chives

⅓ cup Cilantro

Sea Salt (to taste)

Rinse the kelp noodles in water and cut to desired length. Chop the chives and cilantro, add to the kelp noodles, and set aside for later.

Combine coconut aminos, coconut vinegar, maple syrup, garlic, ginger, and sesame oil and blend until smooth. Make sure there are no remaining chunks; if you are unsure, strain it. You don't want to surprise anyone with a piece of raw garlic!

Add the coconut aminos mixture to the kelp noodles, toss, and season with sea salt to your liking.

Serves 2 to 4

This recipe is Vegan

POMEGRANATE APPLE SALAD

2 cups Baby Spinach

2 cups Mixed Spring Greens

½ Gala Apple

¼ cup Pomegranate Seeds

¼ cup Toasted Pecans

¼ cup Butternut Squash

2 Tbsp Green Onions

3 Mint Leaves

Sesame Ginger Salad
Dressing (see below)

Optional: Sesame Orange
Roasted Duck

In a bowl, combine the spinach, mixed greens, chopped apple, pomegranate seeds, chopped toasted pecans, diced butternut squash, chopped green onions (I use the green part only), and chopped duck and toss in dressing.

Tip If you plan to toast your own pecans, heat a pan over medium-high heat (~7). Then add the pecans and 1 teaspoon of honey. Toast until browned.

Tip We like to make this salad after making our Sesame Orange Roasted Duck. See our blog at www.paleoeffect.com for the recipe!

Serves 2 to 4

This recipe is Vegan

SESAME GINGER SALAD DRESSING

1 ½ Tbsp Sesame Oil

1 Tbsp Coconut
Vinegar

1 Tbsp Ginger

1 Tbsp Coconut
Aminos

1 ½ Tbsp Honey

¼ cup Olive Oil

2 cloves Garlic

Combine all ingredients and blend until smooth and incorporated.

Tip Try over our delicious Pomegranate Apple Salad!

This recipe is Vegan

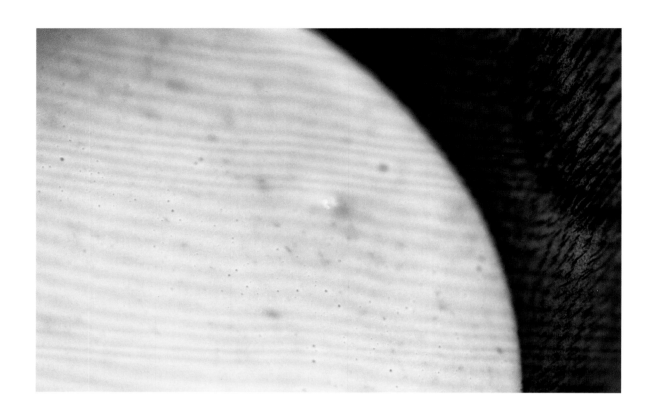

JAPANESE GINGER
SALAD DRESSING

½ cup Grape-Seed Oil	Juice of 1 Lemon	2 tsp Honey
½ cup Olive Oil	3 cloves Garlic	1 Small Carrot
2 Tbsp Coconut Aminos	2 Tbsp Ginger	¼ tsp Coconut Vinegar
	1 tsp Ground Mustard	

Blend all ingredients in a blender or food processor until smooth and incorporated.

This recipe is Vegan

STRAWBERRY AND TOMATO
RED SALAD

2 Campari or Roma
Tomatoes

8 Fresh Basil Leaves

1 pint Strawberries

Balsamic Glaze
(see page 18)

Sea Salt and Black Pepper
(to taste)

Dice the tomatoes and strawberries, discarding the tops (discarding the stems and leaves). Cut the basil into small, ¼" strips. Toss the tomatoes, basil, and strawberries together with a pinch of sea salt and black pepper.

Plate and top with balsamic glaze, which will give this salad a rustic sweetness.

Serves 2 to 4

This recipe is Vegan

SWEET POPPY SEED SALAD

1 cup Broccoli florets	*Sweet Poppy Seed Salad Dressing:*	1 tsp Paprika
1 cup Cauliflower florets		2 Tbsp Lemon Juice
1 cup White Button Mushrooms	½ cup Coconut Milk	1 Tbsp Poppy Seeds
	2 Tbsp Water	1 Tbsp Dried Onion Flakes
½ cup Carrots	¼ cup Coconut Crystals	1 tsp Ground Mustard
½ cup Red Onion	⅓ cup Coconut Vinegar	

Combine the coconut milk, water, coconut crystals, coconut vinegar, paprika, lemon juice, onions flakes, and ground mustard and blend until smooth in consistency. Stir in the poppy seeds.

Slice the mushrooms, carrots, and red onion. Toss the salad dressing with the sliced vegetables and the broccoli and cauliflower florets, and serve.

Serves 2 to 4

This recipe is Vegan

RANCH SALAD DRESSING

¼ cup Mayonnaise
   (see page 14)

¼ cup Coconut Milk

1 tsp Dill

½ tsp Garlic Powder

¼ tsp Onion Powder

¼ tsp Chives

1 Tbsp Lemon Juice

Sea Salt and Black Pepper
   (to taste)

Combine all ingredients and blend until smooth and incorporated.

This recipe is Vegetarian

CURRIED CHICKEN SALAD

1 ½ lbs Chicken Breast	¼ cup Celery	2 Tbsp Green Onions
Adobo Seasoning (see page 14)	2 Tbsp Dried Cranberries	¼ cup Pecans
1 cup Chicken Stock	1 ½ tsp Madras Yellow Curry Powder	¼ cup Mayonnaise (see page 14)
Water	1 tsp Lime Juice	Sea Salt (to taste)
¼ cup Green Peppers	¾ cup Honeycrisp Apple	

Dust the chicken with Adobo Seasoning on all sides. Place the chicken in a saucepan, add the chicken stock, and fill with water until the chicken is covered.

Bring the chicken to a boil and cook for 3–5 minutes on high (depending on thickness). After 3–5 minutes, take the chicken off the heat, cover it, and let sit 10–12 minutes or until no longer pink inside. Take the chicken out of the water and let it cool. Then dice it and add it to a bowl.

Dice the green peppers, celery, apple (peel as well), green onions (discard the white parts), and pecans and add to the chicken. Combine with the cranberries, lime juice, Mayonnaise, and sea salt.

Refrigerate overnight if you like, or serve immediately. We actually like this a little better after the flavors have mingled overnight.

Serve in a romaine lettuce boat or on our delicious Fluffy Paleo Bread (see page 35)!

Serves 4 to 6

TUNA SALAD

12 oz Cooked Tuna	½ tsp Coconut Vinegar	¼ tsp Cayenne Powder
1 stalk Celery	½ tsp Lemon Juice	Sea Salt and Black Pepper (to taste)
1 Shallot	1 Tbsp Stone-Ground Mustard	
1 clove Garlic		*Optional:* Paleo Crostini
3 Tbsp Mayonnaise (see page 14)	1 tsp Dill	*Optional:* Tomato
	½ tsp Parsley	*Optional:* Red Onion
6 Tbsp Dill Pickle Relish OR	½ tsp Onion Powder	*Optional:* Lettuce

Dice the celery, onion, and garlic and place in a large bowl.

Combine all remaining ingredients and serve with tomato, lettuce, and onion, or by itself!

Tip We make our own pickle relish by making Refrigerator Dill Pickles (see page 19) and dicing the ingredients! If you make this, you do not need to use any of the ingredients in the middle column or the cayenne pepper.

Tip We like to serve this on our toasted Fluffy Paleo Bread (see page 35) or Paleo Crostini for a delicious sandwich! See our blog at www.paleoeffect.com for more recipes!

Serves 2 to 4

This recipe is Pescatarian

CHICKEN SALAD

1 ½ lbs Chicken Breast

Adobo Seasoning
  (see page 14)

1 cup Chicken Stock

Water

1 cup Celery

½ cup Mayonnaise
  (see page 14)

1 Tbsp Dijon Mustard

2 Green Onions

¼ cup Walnuts

2 Tbsp Tarragon

1 cup Red Grapes

1 Tbsp Lemon Juice

1 Tbsp Olive Oil

Sea Salt and Black Pepper
  (to taste)

¼ cup Parsley

Fluffy Paleo Bread Slices
  (see page 35)

Tomato Slices

Romaine Lettuce

Red Onions

Dust the chicken with Adobo Seasoning on all sides. Place the chicken in a saucepan, add the chicken stock, and fill with water until the chicken is covered.

Bring the chicken to a boil and cook for 3–5 minutes on high (depending on thickness). After 3–5 minutes, take the chicken off the heat, cover it, and let sit 10–12 minutes or until no longer pink inside. Take the chicken out of the water and let it cool. Then dice it and add it to a bowl.

In another bowl, combine the diced celery, Mayonnaise mustard, green onions, walnuts, tarragon, lemon juice, halved grapes, sea salt, and black pepper. Cut the chicken into ½" cubes and fold it and the olive oil into the Mayonnaise mixture.

Next, toast some of our Fluffy Paleo Bread in the oven at 350 degrees Fahrenheit for about 5–10 minutes, then top with lettuce (or just use the lettuce as a bowl if you don't want the bread), tomato, red onion, and chopped parsley.

Serves 4 to 6

SIDES

Twice-Baked Broccoli Casserole • Hush Puppies • Chinese Fried "Rice" • Savory Grits with Bacon
Asian-Inspired Slaw • Creamy Coleslaw • Apple Curry Slaw • Colcannon • Wilted Kale
Lemon Garlic Asparagus • Roasted Creole Okra • Mofongo • Cranberry Sauce
Ginger-Glazed Carrots • Sweet Potato Casserole • Celery and Herb Stuffing
Sweet Potato Salad • Garlic Mashed Sweet Potatoes
Sautéed Zucchini and Summer Squash • Au Gratin Sweet Potatoes

TWICE-BAKED BROCCOLI CASSEROLE

1 head Cauliflower florets	1 cup Broccoli florets	¼ cup Chives
¼ cup Coconut Milk	2 strips Bacon	1 cup Baby Spinach
½ Tbsp Walnut Oil	⅓ cup Sweet Onion	Sea Salt and Black Pepper (to taste)
1 Tbsp Olive Oil	1 clove Garlic	

Preheat the oven to 350 degrees Fahrenheit.

Bring ½ cup water to a boil and add the cauliflower florets. Turn the heat down to medium (~5) and steam, partially covered, for about 8 minutes.

In a food processor, combine the cauliflower, coconut milk, and walnut oil and season with a little sea salt and black pepper. Blend until *very* smooth and silky.

Next, steam the broccoli. The same method should work just fine.

As the broccoli is steaming, heat the olive oil in a pan over medium-high heat (~6). Once hot, add the diced bacon and diced sweet onion. Sauté the onions and bacon until the onions are caramelized (i.e., they have a nice brown tint).

Once caramelized, add the minced garlic and sliced baby spinach. Cook the mixture for another minute, or until the garlic is fragrant.

Add the broccoli and onion mixture to the cauliflower and pulse until all ingredients are incorporated. Some chunks are good—or at least, we like it that way. Blend to your liking.

Once blended, stir in the chopped chives, reserving a little for garnish.

Pour the mixture into a baking dish and bake, uncovered, for 22–25 minutes, or until the casserole turns a golden brown at the peaks.

Serves 4

This recipe can easily be made Vegan; just omit the bacon

HUSH PUPPIES

2 Green Plantains

1 Egg

¼ cup Red Onion

¼ cup Red Bell Pepper

¼ cup Breadcrumbs
(see page 15)

2 Tbsp Carrots

1 small clove Garlic

1 Green Onion

½ Tbsp Coconut Oil

1 tsp Sea Salt

½ tsp Black Pepper

Coconut Oil (for frying)

These are going to be so easy, you won't believe that you ever bought them at the store! First, put some sea-salted water on the stove to boil.

Peel the green plantains: cut the ends off, run a knife along the peel, get your fingernails under there, and peel the outside off. This will not be like peeling a banana; it will be harder.

Cut the plantains into 3" chunks and add to the boiling water. Boil for 10 minutes. Drain.

Now here's the easy part if you have a food processor. Add the plantains, egg, red onion, red bell pepper, Breadcrumbs carrots, garlic, green onion (sans the white part), ½ tablespoon coconut oil, sea salt, and black pepper. Keep pulsing until all ingredients are well incorporated. If you don't have a food processor, you'll want to mash the plantains as best you can, mince everything else, and combine.

Now we want to take about 2 tablespoons and roll it into a ball. I like to roll all of these up before I start frying; it keeps the ball moving (haha, pun intended?), and I don't have to stop in the middle to make more.

Heat the coconut oil over medium-high heat (~8). Drop a little piece of batter into the oil to test. If it immediately starts sizzling, we're good to go. Drop hush puppies in one layer in the oil and cook for about 4–5 minutes or until golden brown and done all the way through.

Tip The green plantains *must* be green. Not a little yellow, not brown, and definitely *not* black. Green. Very, very green.

Makes 18 to 20

This recipe is Vegetarian

CHINESE FRIED "RICE"

1 head Cauliflower	3 Tbsp Coconut Aminos	1 tsp Red Pepper Flakes
2 Tbsp Sesame Oil	1 Egg	½ White Onion
4 Green Onions	6 cloves Garlic	

Grate the cauliflower in a food processor (or by hand) until it resembles rice.

Once the cauliflower is riced, heat the sesame oil over medium-high heat (~7). Add the diced white onion, the minced garlic, and the cauliflower. Let it brown a little, then reduce the heat to medium (~4) and add the chopped green onions, coconut aminos, and red pepper flakes.

Cook for another 2 minutes, then add the egg. We literally just crack the egg into the pan with the cauliflower and mix it around until it is cooked through.

Keep over medium heat (~4) until the cauliflower is tender. The way we like ours, it takes about 6–7 minutes. If you want this to cook faster, cover the pan while it cooks.

Tip If you like contrasting textures, you can chop some water chestnuts very finely to give it a little crunch. We'd suggest using ¼ cup, added at the same time as the cauliflower.

Serves 2 to 4

This recipe is Vegetarian but can easily be made Vegan; just omit the egg

SAVORY GRITS WITH BACON

3 cups Grated Cauliflower	1 strip Bacon	½ tsp Sea Salt (or to taste)
1 Tbsp Walnut Oil	2 cloves Garlic	½ tsp Black Pepper (or to taste)
⅔ cup Coconut Milk	1 ½ Tbsp Arrowroot Powder	pinch Sage
⅔ cup Beef Stock (reserve 2 Tbsp for slurry)	+ 2 Tbsp Beef Stock (= slurry)	

Food process or mince the cauliflower so it resembles the texture of grits. Then dice the bacon and mince the garlic.

Heat the oil over medium-high (~7) and add the bacon. Cook until the bacon reaches your desired crispiness then add the garlic and cook until fragrant (about 1 minute).

Turn the heat down to medium (~5). Mix in the cauliflower, coconut milk, and stock. Cover and cook for 12–15 minutes, stirring occasionally.

Season the mixture with sea salt and black pepper. Once you have it seasoned, add sage to taste. It will not take much sage!

Mix the 2 tablespoons of beef stock with the arrowroot in a cup or bowl. Then add the slurry to the cauliflower mixture. Keep uncovered and cook on medium until thick and creamy and all cauliflower is tender.

Serves 2 to 4

This recipe can easily be made Vegan; just swap the beef stock with vegetable stock and omit the bacon

ASIAN-INSPIRED SLAW

½ tsp Red Pepper Flakes	1 Tbsp Coconut Aminos	1 Carrot
1 clove Garlic	2 tsp Coconut Oil	½ cup Broccoli
¼ cup Coconut Vinegar	½ tsp Sea Salt	2 Tbsp Cucumber
1 tsp Honey	3 cups Napa Cabbage	3 Green Onions

Combine the first 7 ingredients and refrigerate for 15 minutes.

While the marinade is in the refrigerator, shred the napa cabbage, carrot, broccoli, and cucumber. Dice the green onions, reserving a few for garnish. Add these ingredients to the marinade and let rest for another 15 minutes. Garnish with green onions and serve!

Tip We suggest that you use an English (or Hothouse) cucumber. They are less watery and have fewer seeds.

Serves 4 to 6

This recipe is Vegan

CREAMY COLESLAW

½ head Cabbage

¼ cup Red Onion

½ cup Carrots

1 Tbsp Coconut Crystals

3 Tbsp Coconut Vinegar

1 Tbsp Cilantro

¼ cup Mayonnaise
(see page 14)

½ Tbsp Poppy Seeds

Sea Salt and Black Pepper
(to taste)

This one is an easy one. You just chop the cabbage as fine or as thick as you like. Do the same with the onions and carrots and add them all to a bowl.

Next, combine the coconut crystals, coconut vinegar, cilantro, Mayonnaise, poppy seeds, sea salt, and black pepper. Once the coconut crystals and sea salt are dissolved, add to the vegetables.

Put the coleslaw in the refrigerator and chill for at least 30 minutes, which will allow the flavors to mingle and the cabbage to slightly soften.

Serves 4

This recipe is Vegetarian

APPLE CURRY SLAW

⅔ cup Coconut Milk

2 Tbsp Green Curry Paste

2 tsp Lemongrass

½ tsp Madras Yellow Curry Powder

1 Tbsp Honey

1 Tbsp Lime Juice

½ tsp Sea Salt

½ tsp Ginger

2 tsp Coconut Vinegar

1 cup Gala Apples

1 ½ cups Green Cabbage

1 cup Shredded Carrots

1 cup Broccoli Slaw

½ cup Red Cabbage

¼ cup Roasted Sunflower Seeds

Combine the coconut milk, green curry paste, lemongrass, yellow curry powder, honey, lime juice, sea salt, ginger, and coconut vinegar in a bowl big enough for all ingredients and mix until incorporated.

Peel and cut the apples into matchsticks. We want everything to blend, so even sizes are best.

Next, add the red and green cabbages, carrots, broccoli slaw, and apples to the coconut milk mixture.

Garnish with sunflower seeds and serve cold.

Tip Broccoli slaw is sold in many grocery stores, but few have it organic. If you want to go organic (and we always recommend it), buy the whole broccoli, cut off the florets and save for later, then shred the stems. Waste not, want not!

Serves 4

This recipe is Vegan

COLCANNON

1 lb Parsnips	3 strips Bacon	¼ cup Coconut Milk
1 Tbsp Olive Oil	1 Small White Onion	Sea Salt and Black Pepper (to taste)
2 cups Kale	2 Tbsp Chicken Stock	Green Onions

Preheat the oven to 400 degrees Fahrenheit.

Peel and roughly chop the parsnips into ½" pieces, discarding the tops and tips. Toss with olive oil, sea salt, and black pepper. We use roughly ½ teaspoon of each. Then spread out on a baking sheet and bake in the middle rack for about 20-25 minutes or until fork tender.

As the parsnips are cooking, dice the bacon and cook in a pan over medium-high heat (~7) until desired crispiness is achieved. We like for it to have a little crunch.

Once the bacon is crispy, remove it from the fat and set aside for later.

But wait! Save that bacon fat! We're going to use it. So place the pan with the fat back on the burner and add the diced onion (i.e., about a cup).

Cook the onions until browned and cara-melized. Then remove them from the pan and set aside with the bacon.

But wait! We're still using the fat! Remove the ribs from the kale, dice kale into small pieces, and add it to the pan. Turn the heat way down to medium-low (~4), cover, and cook until the kale is tender (about 5 minutes).

Add the kale, any leftover bacon fat, coconut milk, and chicken stock to the bacon and onions. When the parsnips are ready, add them to the kale mixture and mash the mixture until it is the con-sistency you want. We like ours a little chunkier, but if you use a hand mixer, you can get yours nice and creamy.

Season with sea salt and black pepper (to taste) and garnish with diced green onions.

Tip This recipe is great alongside our Corned Beef and Cabbage! (see page 130)

Serves 4

This recipe can easily be made Vegan; just swap the chicken stock with vegetable stock and omit the bacon

WILTED KALE

8 cups Kale	4 Tbsp Pine Nuts	4 Tbsp Olive Oil
½ cup Water	2 cloves Garlic	Sea Salt and Black Pepper (to taste)
2 Tomatoes	2 Tbsp Lemon Juice	

In a bowl big enough to fit all ingredients, combine the minced garlic, lemon juice, olive oil, chopped tomato, and pine nuts.

Heat the water in a pan over medium-high heat (~7). Once bubbles begin to form in the water, add the kale (cut into manageable pieces) and reduce the heat to medium (~5). Cover and cook for 5 minutes, tossing every so often to ensure even cooking.

Once wilted, remove from heat and drain the excess water. Add the kale to the garlic and lemon juice mixture and toss to coat. Season with sea salt and black pepper and serve immediately.

Serves 4

This recipe is Vegan

LEMON GARLIC ASPARAGUS

1 bunch Asparagus

2 Tbsp Olive Oil

2 cloves Garlic

2 tsp Lemon Juice

Sea Salt (to taste)

pinch White Pepper

Pinch Cayenne Powder

Preheat the oven to 375 degrees Fahrenheit.

Trim the asparagus bottoms. Mince the garlic and toss with the asparagus, oil, lemon, cayenne, sea salt, and white pepper. Spread the asparagus out on a baking sheet or grill pan.

Bake for 15 minutes, uncovered, turning the asparagus once for even cooking.

Serves 2 to 4

This recipe is Vegan

ROASTED CREOLE OKRA

24 Okra

2 Tbsp Almond Flour

1 Tbsp Adobo Seasoning (see page 14)

½ Tbsp Olive Oil

½ Tbsp Walnut Oil

2 tsp Creole Seasoning

1 tsp Lemon Juice

½ tsp Sea Salt

½ tsp Black Pepper

Preheat the oven to 400 degrees Fahrenheit.

Let the okra come to room temperature. While that happens, combine the almond flour, Adobo Seasoning, Creole seasoning, sea salt, and black pepper in a bowl.

Once the okra is at room temperature, toss it with the olive oil, walnut oil, and lemon juice. Next, add the almond flour mixture and toss to coat.

Lay the okra in a single layer on baking sheets. We use parchment paper, but if you don't have any, greasing a baking pan will work fine as well. You don't want to overcrowd them, so give them each their own space.

Bake for 12 minutes, then broil for another 2–3 minutes, or or until golden brown.

Tip This recipe is great with our Jambalaya! (see page 155)

Serves 4

This recipe is Vegan

MOFONGO

6 Green Plantains

2 Tbsp Adobo Seasoning
(see page 14)

4 cloves Garlic

¼ cup + 1 Tbsp Olive Oil

¼ cup Chicken Stock

Coconut Oil

Sea Salt

Optional: ½ cup Pork Rinds

Peel the green plantains. This should be a little difficult: cut the tops and bottoms off, then run a knife down the length of one side. Get your fingers under and peel. Once all of the plantains are peeled and put in a bowl, cover them with cold water and add sea salt until the plantains float. Let the plantains sit in the water for at least 20 minutes. Sometimes, we'll leave them overnight, but no longer than one day. When ready, drain the water and cut the plantains into 1" pieces.

Heat the coconut oil to high. Dry the plantains, then add them to the oil and fry them until they are a golden brown. Once golden brown, remove from oil and drain on a paper towel.

Heat the 1 tablespoon of olive oil in a sauté pan over medium-high heat and add the minced garlic. Sauté the garlic for just one minute, stirring constantly, then transfer to a bowl or a pestle and mortar. Add to the garlic the remaining olive oil, pork rinds, chicken stock, and plantains. These will be hard to mash, but it must be done. If you can't mash them with a hand masher, you may have to food-process them.

Serves 6

This recipe can easily be made Vegan; just swap the chicken stock with vegetable stock and omit the pork rinds

CRANBERRY SAUCE

12 oz Cranberries	1 tsp Ginger	*Optional:* pieces of
1 cup Orange Juice	½ tsp Orange Zest	Mandarin Orange
½ cup Honey	pinch Cinnamon	

Mince the ginger and orange zest. Boil the orange juice, ginger, and orange zest on high heat.

Once the liquid is boiling, add the cranberries. Reduce heat to medium (~4) and cook uncovered for 7–10 minutes, stirring occasionally until the cranberries have burst open.

Remove the cranberries from the heat and add the honey and cinnamon. Stir and set aside to cool. Once the cranberry sauce reaches room temperature, cover and refrigerate. This recipe can be made several days in advance.

This recipe is Vegan

GINGER-GLAZED CARROTS

3 Tbsp Sesame Oil	2 Tbsp Ginger	6 cloves Garlic
8 Carrots	½ cup Green Onion	1 tsp Sea Salt

Preheat the oven to 400 degrees Fahrenheit.

Mince the garlic and ginger. Chop the green onions. Cut the carrots into ¼" spears (about 3" long) or matchsticks.

Add all ingredients except for the oil to a bowl and toss with the carrots.

Heat the oil in a pan on high until it begins to smoke.

Once the oil is hot, add the oil to the remaining ingredients and toss until thoroughly coated.

Spread the carrots and all of the contents of the bowl out onto a baking sheet.

Bake the spears for 25–35 minutes, or until tender. If you went the matchsticks route, bake for only 12–15 minutes.

Serves 4

This recipe is Vegan

SWEET POTATO CASSEROLE

2 Large Sweet Potatoes

1 Honeycrisp Apple

¼ cup Apple Juice

pinch Allspice

2 Tbsp Coconut Crystals

2 tsp Arrowroot Powder

2 Eggs

½ cup Coconut Crystals

½ tsp Sea Salt

¼ cup Coconut Oil

¼ cup Coconut Milk

2 tsp Vanilla Extract

Topping:

½ cup Coconut Crystals

¼ cup Coconut Flour

¾ cup Walnuts

3 Tbsp Coconut Oil

½ tsp Cinnamon

Preheat the oven to 350 degrees Fahrenheit.

Peel and dice the sweet potatoes into large chunks and boil them in water for about 20 minutes or until soft.

While the sweet potatoes are boiling, peel and dice the apple. Add the apples, allspice, coconut crystals, and arrowroot powder to a saucepan over medium heat (~5) and cook, covered, for 5 minutes. You will want to stir the apples occasionally until tender.

Combine the sautéed apples, eggs, coconut crystals, sea salt, coconut oil, coconut milk, and vanilla extract in a food processor or blender and blend until smooth.

Combine the sweet potatoes and the apple mixture and mash until the sweet potatoes are the desired texture.

Pour the sweet potato mixture into a greased, 8" x 8" glass baking dish.

In a separate bowl, combine all topping ingredients. If you are using coconut oil that is solid, you will want to heat it to liquefy it first. Once the ingredients are mixed thoroughly, spread the topping out over the sweet potatoes.

Bake, uncovered, for 35 minutes.

Tip Looking for more Thanksgiving Day recipes? Go to our blog at www.paleoeffect.com!

Serves 4 to 6

This recipe is Vegetarian

CELERY AND HERB STUFFING

1 loaf Fluffy Paleo
    Bread (see
    page 35)

2 Tbsp Walnut Oil

2 stalks Celery

¼ White Onion

1 clove Garlic

¼ cup White Wine
    (or Water)

14 oz Chicken Stock

1 Egg

¼ cup Parsley

2 sprigs Thyme

1 sprig Rosemary

¼ tsp Sage

½ tsp Sea Salt

½ tsp Black Pepper

You can make the bread in advance, dice into ½" cubes, and set it out to dry a little. It is better if it is a little stale.

Preheat the oven to 400 degrees Fahrenheit.

Spread the bread out on a baking sheet and bake for 10 minutes, or if you made it the same day, 15 minutes or until slightly crunchy.

In a saucepan, heat the walnut oil on medium-high heat (~7). Chop the celery, onion, garlic, sea salt, and black pepper and add to the hot oil. Cook until soft, about 5–7 minutes. Add the white wine (or water) and cook until evaporated.

In a separate bowl large enough for all ingredients, combine the onion mixture, eggs (don't mix them when the onions are too hot or it will cook the eggs!), parsley, rosemary, sage, thyme, and bread.

Mix in half of the stock stirring the stuffing. You want the bread to be moist, but not wet. If it takes all of the stock, then use it; if it doesn't, then don't. We usually use about 8 ounces of stock.

Grease an 8" x 8" glass baking dish with a little walnut oil. Spoon the stuffing into the dish and cover with tin foil.

Bake, covered, for 25 minutes. Then uncover and bake for another 10–15 minutes, or until golden on the top.

Tip This recipe can be made ahead of time; just follow the recipe up to the "cover with tin foil" part, then refrigerate until you are ready to cook.

Tip For more Thanksgiving Day recipes, visit our blog at www.paleoeffect.com!

Serves 4 to 6

This recipe can easily be made Vegetarian; just swap the chicken stock with vegetable stock

SWEET POTATO SALAD

2 Large Sweet Potatoes	1 ½ Tbsp Coconut Vinegar	¼ cup Parsley
2 Tbsp Extra Virgin Olive Oil	½ tsp Ground Chipotle Pepper	3 Green Onions
¼ cup Mayonnaise (see page 14)	1 tsp Ground Mustard	3 strips Bacon + Reserved Fat
	1 tsp Honey	Sea Salt and Black Pepper (to taste)
2 Dried Arbol Chili Peppers		

Preheat the oven to 400 degrees Fahrenheit.

Cut the sweet potatoes (leaving the skins on) into cubes (about a ½" to 1"). Toss with 2 tablespoons of olive oil, sea salt, and black pepper. Spread the sweet potatoes out on a baking sheet and cook for 20 minutes, or until they are tender.

While the sweet potatoes are cooking, blend together the Mayonnaise arbol chili peppers, coconut vinegar, chipotle pepper, ground mustard, and honey. Blend until well incorporated. Set aside.

Dice and cook the bacon (to the crispiness of your liking). Chop the parsley and green onions, discarding the stems and white parts.

When the potatoes are done, mix all ingredients together. If you like potato salad warm, serve it immediately. If you like it cold, place it in the refrigerator and let it chill. This recipe keeps well, so it can also be made a day in advance.

Serves 2 to 4

This recipe can easily be made Vegetarian; just omit the bacon

GARLIC MASHED SWEET POTATOES

3 cups Diced Sweet Potatoes

2 cloves Garlic

2 Tbsp Extra Virgin Olive Oil

Sea Salt and Black Pepper
(to taste)

⅓ cup Coconut Milk

1 tsp Herbes de Provence

1 tsp Lemon Juice

⅛ tsp Cayenne Powder

Preheat the oven to 400 degrees Fahrenheit.

Toss the diced sweet potatoes (with the skins still on, so be sure to wash them first) with the garlic, oil, sea salt, and black pepper. Spread out on a baking sheet and cook for 25 minutes, shaking once or twice to rotate. The potatoes should be very soft.

While your potatoes are in the oven, combine the coconut milk, herbs, lemon juice, and cayenne. Make sure that your herbs are well ground or else you'll crunch on pieces of them when you eat. And nobody wants that, trust me.

When the sweet potatoes are done, put all ingredients in a food processor and blend until smooth. Don't have one? No worries, you can use a hand mixer or go old-fashioned and mash all ingredients together until you reach the desired consistency. Add sea salt and black pepper if you need to adjust the seasoning, and serve.

Serves 2

This recipe is Vegan

SAUTÉED ZUCCHINI AND SUMMER SQUASH

2 Zucchini	½ Tbsp Walnut Oil	2 Dried Arbol Chili Peppers
1 Yellow Squash	Sea Salt and Black Pepper (to taste)	6-8 drops Lemon Juice
1 Tbsp Olive Oil		

First, slice the zucchini into ¼" slices. Next, slice the squash slightly thicker than the zucchini. Squash cooks faster than zucchini, so if you want to throw them in the same pan, you need to even out the cook time by thickening the slices of squash.

Heat the olive oil in a pan over medium-high heat (~7). Then season the vegetables with the remaining ingredients and add to the hot pan.

Stir until thoroughly coated, cover for 4–6 minutes, then uncover and cook for another 2–4 minutes. It takes a little longer than when covering the pan, but it keeps the gourds from getting too soggy.

This recipe is Vegan

AU GRATIN SWEET POTATOES

2 Sweet Potatoes

½ cup Sweet Yellow
  Onion

1 cup Coconut Milk

3 strips Bacon + Re-
  served Fat

½ Tbsp Olive Oil

1 tsp Lemon Juice

1 tsp Sea Salt

½ tsp Black Pepper

½ tsp Cayenne
  Powder

¼ tsp Garlic Powder

2 Tbsp Arrowroot
  Powder

1 Tbsp Water

Preheat the oven to 475 degrees Fahrenheit.

First, mix the arrowroot powder with the 1 tablespoon water until incorporated. Then blend together the coconut milk, lemon juice, sea salt, black pepper, cayenne, garlic powder, and arrowroot mixture until smooth.

Dice the bacon and onions. Heat the olive oil over medium-high heat (~7) and add the bacon and onions to it. Cook until the onions are slightly translucent. Once finished, let cool for just a moment, then add to the coconut milk mixture and stir to incorporate.

Peel and slice the sweet potatoes to be about ⅛" thick. I like to use a food processor, but a mandolin will work well too. The key is not to slice them too thickly or else they'll have to be in the oven forever.

Lay down a layer in your baking dish. Then pour a little coconut milk mixture. Then a layer of sweet potatoes, then the coconut mixture. Do this until both are used or you run out of room. I like to save a little of the bacon and onion for the top.

Cover with tin foil and bake for 45 minutes. Depending on how thick your slices are, you may want to poke the middle with a knife; it should slide in easily, with no effort.

Let it sit uncovered for 5–10 minutes to set, then serve.

This recipe can easily be made Vegan; just omit the bacon

GRASS FED

Teriyaki Skirt Steak • Spaghetti and Meatballs • Corned Beef and Cabbage • Shepherd's Pie
Vietnamese Steak • Asian Beef Lettuce Wraps • Meatloaf
Pot Roast • Paleo Effect Signature Burger • Lamb and Cauliflower Curry
Braised Lamb Shoulder with Butternut Squash Mash

TERIYAKI SKIRT STEAK

1 lb Skirt Steak

Adobo Seasoning
(see page 14)

2 Tbsp Green Onions

1 Tbsp Olive Oil

¼ cup Beef Stock

Teriyaki Sauce
(see page 51)

Lightly dust the skirt steak with the Adobo Seasoning on each side. Heat the olive oil over high heat. Add the meat to the pan, searing for a couple minutes on each side, then add the beef stock and teriyaki sauce.

Broil for 8–10 minutes (depending on the thickness of the meat), flipping once around the 5-minute mark. If you think about it, baste the steak with the sauce as well.

Serves 2 to 4

SPAGHETTI AND MEATBALLS

1 lb Ground Beef	2 Tbsp Water	Tomato Sauce with
½ cup Breadcrumbs	3 Tbsp Sweet Yellow Onion	Mushrooms
(see page 15)	1 Tbsp Sweet Chili Sauce	(see page 52)
1 Egg	(see page 18)	1 Spaghetti Squash

Preheat the oven to 375 degrees Fahrenheit.

As the oven is heating, prepare the Tomato Sauce with Mushrooms.

Cut the spaghetti squash in half lengthwise. Scrape out and discard the seeds and stringy/gooey insides. Place the squash cut side down on a baking sheet and bake for 40–45 minutes. Let it cool slightly, then scrape out the insides with a fork. It should look like spaghetti. Place this beautiful squash in a serving bowl and set aside.

In a bowl, mix the Breadcrumbs with the egg, water, Sweet Chili Sauce, and minced yellow onion. Then add the beef and mix until thoroughly incorporated. Get in there with your hands to really make sure all of the ingredients are combined.

Roll the meat into 2" balls and place on the greased baking sheet. Bake for 20–25 minutes total, turning at least once around the 10-minute mark. You want to do this, or else your meatballs will turn out flat and weirdly soft and flat on one side.

Serves 4

This recipe can be made Vegan, just omit the meatballs!

CORNED BEEF AND CABBAGE

4 lbs Beef Brisket	*The Brine:*	½ tsp Mustard Seeds	1 ½ tsp Whole Yellow
1 Large Yellow Onion	1 quart Water	3 Whole Cloves	Mustard Seeds
1 lb Carrots	¼ cup Sea Salt	2 cloves Garlic	1 tsp Whole Allspice
1 head Cabbage	2 Tbsp Coconut Vinegar		½ tsp Whole Cloves
2 Large Parsnips	1 Tbsp Honey	*The Simmering Liquid:*	1 tsp Honey
Pickled Mustard Seed	2 Bay Leaves	1 quart Beef Stock + Water	2 Bay Leaves
(see page 53)	1 ½ tsp Whole Peppercorns	(to cover)	4 cloves Garlic
		1 ½ tsp Whole Peppercorns	

Brine: Combine all ingredients in a bag or bowl and add the raw meat. Let rest, refrigerated, for at least 24 hours. Make sure that the meat is completely covered by the liquid. Turn the bag occasionally to make sure the meat is evenly seasoned. You can leave this to soak for a couple of days! After soaking, remove the meat from the brine and discard the liquid.

Heat a large stockpot (or Dutch oven) over high heat and sear the meat on all edges until brown. It should be about 1–2 minutes on each side.

Pour in the stock and then fill the pot with water until the meat is covered. Try to account for evaporation; you do not want the meat to be uncovered at any time or it will dry out, so be generous with your water and cover with at least an inch. Add the rest of the simmering ingredients and bring the stock to a boil. Reduce the heat to medium-low (~3), then cover and cook for 3–4 hours. For 4 pounds, it takes about 4 hours.

During this time, peel the parsnips, carrots, and onion, and remove the outer layers and core of the cabbage. We like to cut the vegetables into big chunks, but you can cut them however you like to eat them (we shoot for 1 onion equals about 8 wedges).

After the 3–4 hours, add the carrots and cook for 10 minutes. Then add the parsnips and cook for 10 minutes. Then add the remaining vegetables and cook for another 10–20 minutes or until tender. Season with sea salt and black pepper (to taste) and garnish with our Pickled Mustard Seed (see page 53)!

Tip Corned Beef should *always* be cut across the grain if you are cutting it, but you won't need to for this recipe. It will pull away with a fork and melt in your mouth!

Tip You can substitute the beef stock with beer if you prefer. Once you cover the meat and add the simmering liquids, skim off the foam from the top.

Serves 6 to 8

SHEPHERD'S PIE

1 lb Ground Beef

Adobo Seasoning
(see page 14)

1 Tbsp Duck Fat

1 Yellow Onion

1 Zucchini

3 Carrots

1 tsp Thyme

2 tsp Arrowroot
Powder

4 oz Tomato Sauce

¼ cup Chicken Stock

Mashed No-tatoes:

1 head Cauliflower

¼ cup Almond Milk
(unsweetened)

½ Tbsp Walnut Oil

Sea Salt and Black
Pepper (to taste)

Preheat the oven to 400 degrees Fahrenheit.

First, let's make the Mashed No-tatoes. Trim the cauliflower, removing the stalks. Bring a ½ cup water to boil in a saucepan. Add the cauliflower florets, turn the heat down to medium (~5), and steam them until tender. Drain the water.

In a bowl or food processor, combine the cauliflower, almond milk, and walnut oil. If you are not using a food processor, mash the ingredients until you reach a whipped consistency. Season with sea salt and black pepper and set aside for later.

Peel and slice the carrots into ¼" discs. Peel and dice the onions and zucchini.

Heat the duck fat over medium-high heat (~7) in a large saucepan. Add the carrots and sauté for 2–3 minutes. Then add the onions and sauté until they caramelize (i.e., turn a light brown). Add the zucchini, arrowroot powder, thyme, sea salt, and black pepper to taste.

Season the meat with Adobo Seasoning (just a light dusting) and cook until no longer pink. Add the tomato sauce and chicken stock. Turn the heat down to medium (~4) and let the sauce reduce for about 10 minutes. Once thickened, transfer the mixture into a greased 8" x 8" glass baking dish.

Pour the Mashed No-tatoes over the meat mixture.

Bake uncovered for 20 minutes, then turn up the heat and broil for 5 minutes or until the top is golden brown.

Tip We use duck fat for its unique flavor, but you can use your preference of fat or oil.

Serves 4 to 6

VIETNAMESE STEAK

2 New York Strip Steaks	½ tsp Black Pepper	1 Tbsp Coconut Oil
1 Tbsp Lemongrass	1 Tbsp Fish Sauce	1 tsp Cilantro
2 cloves Garlic	1 Tbsp Coconut Aminos	2 Dried Arbol Chili Peppers
1 Tbsp Honey	1 Tbsp Lime Juice	1 tsp Ginger

Blend all ingredients except the steak. Combine the mixture with the steak and marinate the meat for at least 20 minutes in the refrigerator. We will let it sit longer if we have the time.

Heat the grill to medium-high. Grill steak about 4 minutes on each side for rare.

Let stand for 5 minutes, then slice thinly against the grain of the meat.

Garnish with cilantro and lime wedges.

Tip See our Perfect Steak Cooking Guide on our blog at www.paleoeffect.com for more tips and tricks to cooking meat!

Serves 2 to 4

ASIAN BEEF LETTUCE WRAPS

2 lbs Ground Beef	3 Dried Arbol Chili Peppers	5 Mushrooms
Adobo Seasoning (see page 14)	1 tsp Honey	½ Yellow Onion
2 tsp Sesame Oil	¼ cup Green Onions	¼ cup Water Chestnuts
1 tsp Olive Oil	1 ½" Ginger	¼ cup Carrots
5 Tbsp Coconut Aminos	1 Tbsp Coconut Vinegar	Romaine Lettuce
4 cloves Garlic	1 cup Napa Cabbage	Sea Salt (to taste)
	1 Red Pepper	

Combine the coconut aminos, garlic, arbol chilies honey, green onion, ginger, and coconut vinegar and blend until smooth and incorporated. Set aside for later.

Heat 1 teaspoon of the sesame oil over medium-high heat in a pan large enough for all the ingredients. Dust the beef with Adobo Seasoning and cook until no longer pink. Pour the meat into a colander to drain the grease.

As the beef is draining, heat the remaining 1 teaspoon of sesame oil and 1 teaspoon of olive oil over medium heat (~5). Slice the onion, pepper, water chestnuts, and mushrooms to about ¼"-thick strips

or chunks (however you want to eat it, really). Add them to the heat and stir-fry until the onions start to turn translucent.

When the onions start to turn translucent, add the beef and sauce into the pan. Cover and cook for 3–4 minutes or until all ingredients are incorporated and warm.

For serving, take a lettuce leaf, add the meat and vegetable mixture, and garnish with fresh cabbage and carrot slices.

Serves 4 to 6

MEATLOAF

1 lb Ground Beef	3 oz Tomato Paste	pinch Ground Chipotle Pepper
¼ cup Almond Flour	1 clove Garlic	
1 Tbsp Arrowroot Powder	½ Tbsp Sea Salt	*Topping:*
¼ Red Onion	1 Basil Leaf	½ cup Ketchup
¼ Carrot	½ tsp Dried Marjoram	1 tsp Cumin
¼ Red Pepper	½ tsp Black Pepper	1 Tbsp Coconut Aminos
¼ Red Chili Pepper	¼ tsp Cayenne Powder	1 Tbsp Honey
¼ cup Mushrooms	½ tsp Chili Powder	pinch Ground Chipotle Pepper
1 Egg	½ tsp Thyme	

Preheat the oven to 350 degrees Fahrenheit. Mix the topping and set aside.

What we do first is get a big bowl and place the meat in it. Next, combine the almond flour, arrowroot powder, red onion, carrot, red pepper, red chili pepper, mushrooms, egg, tomato paste, garlic cloves, sea salt, basil, marjoram, cayenne, chili powder, thyme, and ground chipotle in a food processor and blend until finely chopped. Once chopped, add the vegetables to the meat and mix until incorporated. Don't be afraid to use your hands for this; it will go faster.

Once the mixture is incorporated, get a baking dish or bread loaf pan—yes, this is a great recipe to utilize that old bread loaf pan. Grease the pan with a little coconut oil and then dump the mixture into it. Form a "log" (haha . . . go Paleo!). It should be the length of the dish and about half the width, or fit the loaf pan exactly.

Then cover your meatloaf with the topping.

Pop it in the oven on the middle rack and bake for about an hour. The middle should be cooked through and the loaf should be set up.

Serves 4

POT ROAST

3 lbs Blade-Cut Pot Roast	2 Carrots	2 Bay Leaves
1 Tbsp Duck Fat	8 White Button Mushrooms	1 sprig Thyme
1 Sweet Onion	½ head Cauliflower	¼ tsp Marjoram
2 cloves Garlic	1 ½ cups Chicken Stock	½ tsp Peppercorns
2 ribs Celery	2 ½ cups Beef Stock	Sea Salt and Black Pepper (to taste)

In a pot big enough for all ingredients, heat the fat over high heat. Rub the pot roast with sea salt and black pepper on all sides. Once the fat is hot, sear the sides of the pot roast until all sides are browned (it should take 1–2 minutes on each side). Then remove it from the heat and set it aside.

Turn the heat down to medium (~5). Quarter the onion, add it to the pot, and stir until it is caramelized (nicely browned, about 3–4 minutes). Peel and dice the carrots, break the cauliflower into large florets, remove the stems from the mushrooms, mince the garlic, and chop the celery ribs (keep everything a little big, but still a good edible size). Add them and cook for just a couple of minutes, until the garlic is fragrant and just barely browned.

Then add the meat and all remaining ingredients to the pot. Reduce the heat to low (about a 2–3 on my oven), cover, and cook until the meat is fork tender. This should take about 3 ½–4 ½ hours. For me, it takes about 4 hours. When the meat is tender, take the lid off and cook another 20–30 minutes, to reduce the stock into a thickened gravy. You can do this the easy way by adding 1 tablespoon of arrowroot as well (if you don't want to wait).

Tip Again, we use duck fat because we like the flavor it adds to the dish, but you can use any oil or fat you prefer.

Serves 6 to 8

PALEO EFFECT SIGNATURE BURGERS

1 lb Ground Beef	Tomato	Mixed Greens
1 tsp Black Cyprus Sea Salt	Red Onion	Avocado
½ tsp Sea Salt	Bacon	4 Portobello Mushrooms
½ tsp Coarse Black Pepper	Mayonnaise	1 Tbsp Olive Oil
½ Tbsp Olive Oil	(see page 14)	1 tsp Balsamic Vinegar

Combine the ground beef, black Cyprus sea salt, sea salt, and coarse black pepper. Season one side of the beef, then flip and season the other. Mix in the olive oil and knead to incorporate.

For Grilling: Heat the grill to high heat, around 400 degrees Fahrenheit. You do not have to coat the meat with oil, as we have already incorporated it into the meat. Grill for 5 minutes on the first side, then flip the burgers and cook for another 5 minutes, leaving the grill open. Then close the grill and cook for an additional 3 minutes for medium-rare. Cook an additional 3 minutes for medium-well, and if you want well done, add another 6 minutes to that.

For Pan Frying:
Heat the pan to medium-high heat (~7) and cook the burgers for 12–15 minutes total, flipping every 2–3 minutes or until cooked throughout and no longer pink in the middle.

As the burgers are cooking, heat a pan over high heat. Cut the bacon in half and cook until crispy. Remove from the heat, but reserve the fat. Add the 1 tablespoon of olive oil and teaspoon of balsamic vinegar. The pan will probably steam, but this is OK.

Remove the stems from the portobello mushrooms and place, gill sides down, in the bacon fat mixture. You will want to cook the mushrooms for 10–12 minutes, covered, flipping every few minutes, until they are tender, depending on the thickness.

Once the burgers and the portobello mushrooms are ready, layer: mushroom, greens, sliced red onion, burger, tomato slices (we like thick ¼" slices), greens, Mayonnaise, and, if you are hungry, another portobello mushroom.

Tip We use baby spinach and arugula.

Serves 4

LAMB AND CAULIFLOWER CURRY

16 Lamb Chops	3 cloves Garlic	1 cup Coconut Milk
Adobo Seasoning (see page 14)	1 Yellow Onion	1 cup Water
2 Tbsp Duck Fat	3 Carrots	1 head Cauliflower
2 Tbsp Curry Powder	2 Arbol Chili Peppers	3 cups Baby Spinach
1 Tbsp Ginger	28 oz Diced Tomatoes	Sea Salt and Black Pepper (to taste)

Mince the ginger and garlic, peel and cut the carrots, dice the onions, slice the spinach, and cut florets from the cauliflower. If you bought a rack of lamb, trim the fat and cut individual chops.

Heat the oil in a large heavy-based saucepan over medium-high (~7) heat. Add onion and cook for about 5 minutes or until the onion softens and begins to turn translucent, then add the garlic and cook, stirring, for 1 minute. Add the carrots, Arbol chili peppers, and ginger and cook for another 5 minutes.

Add the curry and cook, stirring, about 1 minute.

Push the onion mixture to the sides of the pan. Season each side of the lamb with sea salt, black pepper, and a little Adobo Seasoning. Brown the lamb for about 2 minutes on each side.

Once the meat has browned, add the tomatoes, coconut milk, and water and bring to a boil. Reduce heat to medium-low and simmer, uncovered, stirring occasionally, for 25 minutes.

Stir in the cauliflower and cook, covered, stirring occasionally, for about 10 minutes or until the cauliflower is just tender. Add the spinach and stir over low heat until heated through (the spinach will wilt quickly).

Season with sea salt and black pepper, to taste, and serve immediately.

Serves 2 to 4

BRAISED LAMB SHOULDER WITH
BUTTERNUT SQUASH MASH

2 lbs Lamb Shoulder (bone in)	½ cup Dry White Wine (or Water)	3 sprigs Thyme
2 Tbsp Olive Oil	2 cups Water	2 sprigs Rosemary
1 Yellow Onion	3 cloves Garlic	1 Bay Leaf
1 Butternut Squash	2 Sage Leaves	Sea Salt and Black Pepper (to taste)
1 rib Celery		

Let the lamb reach room temperature. Season it with sea salt and black pepper on all sides.

Heat the oil to high heat (~8). When hot, add the lamb. Let the lamb cook for 3 minutes—don't touch it. You can shake the pan a little to make sure it isn't sticking, but otherwise, don't touch it. After 3 minutes, flip it and cook for another 3 minutes. Then take the lamb out of the pan and set aside.

Roughly chop the onion into large chunks. With the juices from the lamb, cook the onion until caramelized. Once caramelized, add the lamb, white wine (or water), ½ teaspoon sea salt, and water to a large pot and bring to a boil. Once boiling, turn the heat down to low (~2), cover, and cook for 15 minutes.

While the lamb is cooking, cut the outer rind and the top and bottom off the squash and cube it into 2" chunks. After the 15 minutes are up, flip the lamb and add the squash, celery (chopped into large chunks), chopped garlic, sage, rosemary, thyme, and bay leaf. We like to push this all below the lamb, so it is all fully immersed in the liquid.

Once you've added all the ingredients, cover and cook for another 30 minutes. The bones should be falling out of the lamb at this point.

Drain the liquids from the squash, onions, and celery. With a hand mixer, food processor, or masher, combine all ingredients until smooth.

Serve 4 to 6

PORK

Pulled Pork • Puerto Rican Pork • Asparagus, Mushrooms, and Pork Stir-Fry
Pork Chops with Ginger and Garlic
Holiday-Spiced Pork Roast with Cranberries and Orange • Christmas Ham

PULLED PORK

3 lbs Boneless Pork Sirloin
  Tip Roast

2 Tbsp Olive Oil

2 cups Apple Cider

⅓ cup Ketchup

1 ½ Tbsp Coconut Vinegar

¼ cup Coconut Crystals

Sweet Chipotle BBQ Sauce
  (see page 50)

Dry Rub:

½ Tbsp Cumin

½ Tbsp Garlic Powder

½ Tbsp Onion Powder

½ Tbsp Chili Powder

½ Tbsp Cayenne Powder

½ Tbsp Sea Salt

1 Tbsp Black Pepper

½ Tbsp Paprika

¼ cup Coconut Crystals

1 Tbsp Adobo Seasoning
  (see page 14)

Preheat the oven to 225 degrees Fahrenheit.

Mix all ingredients of the dry rub in a small bowl. You probably won't need to use all of it, but if you do more than 3 pounds you will need it.

Rub the meat down with the dry rub (we use about half of this for a 3-pound roast). Heat the olive oil over high heat (~8). Once very hot, add the pork. You will want to get a nice brown sear on all sides and this should take about 2–3 minutes on each. Once browned, set aside.

In a baking dish, combine the apple cider, ketchup, coconut vinegar, and coconut crystals. Place the

meat in the apple cider mixture, cover, and bake in the middle rack for about 6 hours.

You will want to flip the meat once an hour, to make sure that it is cooking evenly. Start checking at about 5 ½ hours. You should be able to push on it and it should fall apart. Once you reach this stage, remove the lid and cook for an additional 30 minutes.

Once tender and ready, drain the liquid, then baste with some of our Sweet Chipotle BBQ Sauce.

Serves 6 to 8

PUERTO RICAN PORK

4 Pork Chops

Adobo Seasoning (see page 14)

2 Tbsp Olive Oil

2 cloves Garlic

6 Tbsp Don Ayala's Sofrito
  (see page 20)

8 oz Tomato Sauce

8 oz Water

¼ cup Kalamata Olive Juice

¼ cup Kalamata Olives

4 Bay Leaves

½ Tbsp Culantro and Achiote
  Seasoning (see page 16)

Sea Salt and Black Pepper
  (to taste)

Optional: Roasted Red Peppers

Heat the olive oil over medium-high heat (~7), add the chopped garlic and 4 tablespoons Ayala's Sofrito and sauté for about a minute. Lightly dust the pork with Adobo Seasoning on all sides. Add the pork to the sofrito mixture and sauté for about a minute on each side; the pork should be white on both sides.

Next, add the tomato sauce, water, olives, sea salt, black pepper, bay leaves, Culantro y Achiote Seasoning, 2 additional tablespoons of Ayala's Sofrito, and a dash of Adobo Seasoning.

Turn down the heat to medium (~4) and cook, covered, for about 15 minutes. Then turn the heat down again to low (~2) and cook, covered, for 10 minutes.

If you are using roasted red peppers, add 1 pepper per piece of pork and cook them in the step after you add the second set of Ayala's Sofrito.

Serves 4

ASPARAGUS, MUSHROOMS, AND PORK STIR-FRY

1 lb Pork Chops or Ribs	1 Tbsp Coconut Vinegar	½ cup Coconut Aminos
1 Red Bell Pepper	½ cup Chicken Stock	1 Tbsp Arrowroot Powder + 3 Tbsp Water = slurry
16 Asparagus Spears	2 cloves Garlic	
6 Baby Portobello Mushrooms	2 Tbsp Honey	Sea Salt and Black Pepper (to taste)
Adobo Seasoning (see page 14)	2 Tbsp Olive Oil	Green Onions

Slice the pork into ¼" strips. Lightly dust the pork with Adobo Seasoning and then sprinkle the coconut vinegar over the meat and set aside for later.

Cut the asparagus into 1½" pieces, discarding the bottoms. Slice the mushrooms to ¼"-thick slices and the red bell pepper to 1" pieces. Toss with sea salt and black pepper and set aside.

Combine the chicken stock, garlic, honey, coconut aminos, and arrowroot powder and water. Blend and set aside.

Heat the oil over medium-high heat (~7) in a large pan or wok. Once hot, add the pork. Cook until almost no longer pink.

Add the vegetables to the pork. Cover and cook for about 2 minutes, then add the sauce. Stir to coat, and cook until the asparagus is done (about 2 more minutes covered). You'll be able to tell because the asparagus spears will be bright green and give in a little to light pressure.

Garnish with diced green onions and enjoy!

Tip If you don't have arrowroot powder, it will not affect the flavor of the dish, but the sauce's texture will not be as thick.

Serves 2 to 4

PORK CHOPS WITH GINGER AND GARLIC

4 Pork Chops	2 Tbsp Ginger	¼ cup Chicken Stock
¼ cup Coconut Aminos	3 cloves Garlic	1 Tbsp Sesame Oil
2 Tbsp Honey	3 Green Onions	½ tsp Sea Salt
	2 Tbsp Coconut Vinegar	

Mince the ginger and garlic. Chop the green onions. Add all ingredients to a bag and marinate for 20 minutes.

Remove the pork chops from the marinade.

Heat a pan on high heat. Pour the contents of the bag (i.e., pork plus marinade) into the pan. Sear the pork on each side until the edges where the bones are start to bleed. If using boneless pork chops, sear on each side for 2–3 minutes or until slightly browned.

Heat the oven to broil. After the edges start to bleed on the pork, put the entire pan in the oven, uncovered. Broil for 15 minutes. If you do not have an oven-safe pan, transfer the pork to something you can bake in but will still retain the juices. If using boneless, broil uncovered for 10 minutes total.

Serves 4

HOLIDAY-SPICED PORK ROAST
WITH CRANBERRIES AND ORANGE

2 lbs Sirloin Tip Pork Roast

2 cups Orange Juice

1 cup Cranberries

¼ cup Coconut Crystals

1 Tbsp Coconut Vinegar

5 Dried Arbol Chili Peppers

1 tsp Ground Allspice

½ tsp Ground Cloves

½ tsp Ground Ginger

¼ tsp Cayenne Powder

½ tsp Adobo Seasoning
(see page 14)

¼ tsp Sea Salt

¼ cup Coconut Crystals

Preheat the oven to 250 degrees Fahrenheit. Take the pork out of the refrigerator and let it come to room temperature.

In an 8" x 8" glass baking dish, combine the orange juice, cranberries, coconut crystals, and chopped arbol chili peppers.

In a separate bowl, combine the allspice, cloves, ginger, cayenne, Adobo Seasoning, sea salt, and coconut crystals.

Rub the pork down with the spices and place it in the glass dish with the orange juice mixture.

Cook, uncovered, for 5 hours (flipping the roast every hour) for juicy, sliceable pork roast. If you want a festive pulled pork, just leave it in for another 2 hours. Voilà: juicy delicious holiday pulled pork!

Need sauce? You can pour the leftover juices in a pan and boil them down until reduced by at least half. Then add ½ to 1 tablespoon arrowroot powder and incorporate into the drippings (don't just dump it, as it will clump up; make a slurry and add it to the juices).

Serves 4 to 6

CHRISTMAS HAM

Ham (see directions for lbs)	½ Tbsp Dijon Mustard	1 Pineapple
⅓ cup Coconut Crystals	½ Tbsp Coconut Vinegar	¼ cup Pineapple Juice
1 Tbsp Honey	2 Tbsp Maple Syrup	Whole Cloves

Preheat the oven to 325 degrees Fahrenheit.

Core, peel, and cut the pineapple into rings, reserve the juice, and set aside for later.

Combine the coconut crystals, honey, Dijon mustard, coconut vinegar, maple syrup, and pineapple juice. Set aside for later.

Score the ham in a crisscross pattern, just through the fat. Cook the ham, uncovered, in a shallow baking dish for about 20 minutes per pound. An hour before it should come out, cover it in half the glaze and pop it back in the oven for another 30 minutes.

Next, baste the ham in the remaining glaze and push the whole cloves in between the scores of the ham skin. Then cover with pineapple rings and pop it in the oven for another 30 minutes.

Slice and serve!

Tip For example, we usually shoot for about a 7-pound ham, which cooks for an hour and a half. Then it gets glazed, and then baked for 30 minutes. Then it gets glazed and covered with pineapple, and baked for 30 minutes, for a total of 2½ hours. You do the math!

CAGE FREE

Chicken Pot Pie • "Breaded" Chicken Nuggets • Southwestern Chicken Wraps
Chicken Lettuce Wraps • Chicken Korma • Honey Chicken • Oven-Fried Chicken
Shrimp, Chicken, and Andouille Sausage Jambalaya

CHICKEN POT PIE

2 Chicken Breasts

Adobo Seasoning
(see page 14)

3 Tbsp Extra Virgin
Olive Oil

2 cups Chicken Stock

2 Tbsp Walnut Oil

½ Sweet Onion

2 cloves Garlic

¼ cup Arrowroot Powder

¼ cup Coconut Milk

½ cup Carrots

2 stalks Celery

1 Sweet Potato

1 cup Broccoli Florets

1 tsp Sage

Sea Salt and Black
Pepper (to taste)

Biscuit Topping:

½ cup Almond Flour

¼ Golden Flaxseed Meal

¼ cup Coconut Flour

1 tsp Baking Powder

1 Tbsp Walnut Oil

6 Egg Whites

½ tsp Sea Salt

Coconut Oil

Preheat the oven to 400 degrees Fahrenheit.

Dice the chicken. Then dust the chicken with Adobo Seasoning. Heat 1 tablespoon of the extra virgin olive oil and cook the chicken. Drain the grease and set the chicken aside.

Dice the onions, carrots, celery, and sweet potato (skins on) and mince the garlic.

Heat the rest of the oil over medium high heat (~7) and add the onions and garlic. Cook until the onions are almost translucent, then add the arrowroot powder and incorporate. This should look like a paste. Next, add the chicken stock and coconut milk. Mix thoroughly, then add the remaining vegetables and chicken and season with sea salt and black pepper. Turn the heat down to low (~3).

Cook, covered, until the mix is thick and the vegetables are slightly soft. Spoon into 4 regular, oven-safe ramekins and set them on a baking pan.

Next, we'll make the biscuit topping. In a large bowl, combine the almond flour, flaxseed meal, coconut flour, and baking powder and stir until incorporated.

In a blender, combine the walnut oil, sea salt, and egg whites. Blend until frothy, then add the mixture to the dry ingredients. Try not to mix this too much, just enough so that all ingredients are wet and combined.

Cover the filling from edge to edge with the biscuit mix (about ¼" thick) and pop in the oven for 15 minutes.

After 15 minutes, turn down the heat to 325 degrees Fahrenheit and cook until the biscuits are golden brown and the filling is bubbling out the edges, about 10–15 minutes.

Serves 4 to 6

"BREADED" CHICKEN NUGGETS

2 lbs Chicken Breast	½ cup Almond Flour	1 ½ tsp Black Pepper
1 Egg	2 Tbsp Coconut Crystals	½ tsp Paprika
¼ cup Arrowroot Powder	2 tsp Sea Salt	Honey Mustard Dipping Sauce (see page 49)

Beat one egg in a bowl. Dice the chicken into bite-sized chunks and coat in the egg.

Combine the arrowroot powder, almond flour, coconut crystals, sea salt, black pepper, and paprika into a bowl and stir to incorporate.

Dip the chicken in the egg mixture, then roll it in the dry ingredients to coat.

For Frying: You can fry these, but we prefer not to. If you do, heat your oil to medium-high. Shake the excess flour off of the nuggets and fry for about 5 minutes, until no longer pink in the middle and golden brown.

For Oven Baking: Preheat the oven to 425 degrees Fahrenheit. Grease a baking sheet or line with parchment paper and bake for 8–10 minutes, then flip and cook for another 4–5 minutes, or until no longer pink in the middle and golden brown.

Tip If you'd like to use honey instead of coconut crystals, mix the honey into the egg.

Tip These are great with our Honey Mustard Dipping Sauce!

Serves 2 to 4

SOUTHWESTERN CHICKEN WRAPS

4 Chicken Breasts	1 Tbsp Jalapeños	1 Tbsp Olive Oil
2 Tbsp Adobo Seasoning (see page 14)	¼ cup Parley	Sea Salt and Black Pepper (to taste)
⅛ tsp Ground Chipotle Pepper	¼ tsp Cumin	1 Tomato
2 Green Onions	¼ tsp Coriander	½ Red Onion
1 Small Red Pepper	⅛ tsp Cayenne Powder	Romaine Lettuce
½ cup Spinach	⅛ tsp Chili Powder	Avocado Dressing (see page TK)
	1 clove Garlic	

Preheat the oven to 350 degrees Fahrenheit.

Rub the chicken down with olive oil, Adobo Seasoning, chipotle pepper, sea salt, black pepper, cumin, coriander, chili powder, and cayenne powder. We prefer to combine the spices, then season the chicken.

For Oven Baking: Bake on a greased grill pan for 20 minutes or until no longer pink in the middle.

For Grilling: Preheat the grill to high heat. Grill the thawed chicken breasts for 10 minutes on the first side, then flip and cook for another 5–10 minutes, depending on the thickness of the chicken breasts. They should not be pink in the middle.

While the chicken is cooking, heat a pan over medium heat (~5). Slice the red peppers and sauté them with the minced garlic for about 1 minute or until fragrant. Next, add the sliced spinach and jalapeños.

Take one of the lettuce leaves and line it with Avocado Dressing. Then put down your chicken mixture and garnish with chopped tomatoes, onions, parsley, and green onion.

Tip Our preferred method is grilling, but baking is great as well!

Serves 4 to 6

CHICKEN LETTUCE WRAPS

4 cups Chicken

Adobo Seasoning
(see page 14)

2 Tbsp Coconut Oil

2 cups Diced White Button
Mushrooms

⅔ cup Water Chestnuts

4 cloves Garlic

½ cup Toasted Almond Slices

4 Green Onions

3 Tbsp Honey

2 Tbsp Water

½ cup Coconut Aminos

3 Tbsp Coconut Vinegar

2 tsp Sesame Oil

1 tsp Ground Mustard

8 Dried Arbol Chili Peppers

½ tsp Sea Salt

¼ tsp White Pepper

Romaine Lettuce

Shredded Carrots

Combine the coconut crystals, water, coconut aminos, coconut vinegar, sesame oil, mustard, and de-stemmed, minced arbol chilies. Blend until incorporated.

Heat the coconut oil in a pan over medium-high heat (~7). Lightly dust the chicken with Adobo Seasoning and cook until almost completely cooked through. Drain off the excess grease.

Slice the mushrooms and water chestnuts and dice the green onions (reserving some for garnish). Add the blended sauce, mushrooms, water chestnuts, almond slices, sea salt, and white pepper to the chicken. Cook until the mushrooms and water chestnuts are warm and the chicken is cooked through.

Tear leaves from the lettuce to form bowls. Add some of the chicken mixture to the lettuce and top with a small pile of shredded carrots. Garnish with green onions.

Serves 2 to 4

CHICKEN KORMA

2 Tbsp Coconut Oil

2 Chicken Breasts

Adobo Seasoning
(see page 14)

¼ cup Cashews

½ Yellow Onion

1 ½ tsp Ginger

4 cloves Garlic

1 Small Sweet Potato

4 oz Tomato Sauce

¼ cup Water

3 Carrots

4 Dried Arbol Chili
Peppers

2 tsp Sea Salt

2 Tbsp Red Curry Paste

¾ cup Coconut Milk

1 ½ tsp Coriander

½ tsp Turmeric

1 tsp Lemongrass

pinch Fennel

½ Green Bell Pepper

½ Red Bell Pepper

½ cup Cilantro

Very lightly dust the chicken with the Adobo Seasoning. Heat 1 tablespoon coconut oil in a pan over medium-high heat. Cook the chicken until no longer pink. Set aside to drain on a paper towel.

In the same pan, heat 1 tablespoon oil over medium-high heat (~6), add the diced onion, and cook until almost translucent. Then add the garlic and ginger (both minced). Cook until fragrant (about 1 minute).

Add the diced sweet potato, nuts, sliced carrots, tomato sauce, arbol chilies, and water and cook, covered, for about 5 minutes. Stir it at least once.

When the vegetables are slightly tender, add the sea salt, red curry paste, coconut milk, coriander,

turmeric, lemongrass, fennel, and peppers. We like to mix all of these ingredients (except the peppers) together before we add them to the rest, to make sure they are thoroughly incorporated.

Reduce the heat to low (~2) and cook covered, stirring occasionally, for about another 10 minutes. Then uncover it and cook for another 10 minutes (if you have time as it allows the flavors to mesh together).

Garnish with cilantro.

Serves 2

This recipe can easily be made Vegan; just omit the chicken

HONEY CHICKEN

4 Chicken Breasts	4 Dried Arbol Chili Peppers	1 tsp Sesame Seeds
½ Red Bell Pepper	1 Tbsp Ginger	1 tsp Sesame Oil
½ Green Bell Pepper	3 cloves Garlic	½ Tbsp Olive Oil
5 White Button Mushrooms	3 Tbsp Honey	2 Green Onions
1 cup Broccoli Florets	1 ½ Tbsp Coconut Vinegar	¼ tsp Sea Salt
1 cup Carrot Slices	1 Tbsp Arrowroot Powder	White Pepper (to taste)

Cube the chicken and set aside.

Heat the sesame oil and olive oil over medium-high heat (~7). Cut the red and green bell peppers into chunks and slice the carrots. Add them to the hot oil and sauté for 2–3 minutes, covered.

Next, add the chicken, sliced mushrooms, minced garlic, minced ginger, and broccoli florets and sauté, covered, for another 3–4 minutes or until the broccoli is bright green and slightly tender.

Combine the honey, coconut vinegar, arrowroot powder (or the slurry, if it is easier), sea salt, and white pepper to the meat and vegetables, and sauté, stirring, until thickened.

Garnish with chopped green onions and sesame seeds.

Serves 4 to 6

This recipe can easily be made Vegan; just omit the chicken

OVEN-FRIED CHICKEN

4 Chicken Breasts

1 Egg

¼ cup Coconut Milk

Breadcrumbs
    (see page 15)

⅛ tsp Paprika

⅛ tsp Cayenne
    Powder

⅛ tsp White Pepper

Olive Oil

Preheat the oven to 425 degrees Fahrenheit.

In another bowl, mix the egg and the coconut milk.

In another bowl, mix the Breadcrumbs with the paprika, cayenne, and white pepper. Spread the dry mixture out on a plate.

You will want to dip the chicken breast in the egg mixture, then coat both sides in the Breadcrumbs, then place on a greased grill pan or parchment-lined baking sheet. We like to use the grill pan because it allows for

air to flow under the chicken and for all sides to get nice and crispy, but a baking sheet will do. Just make sure to use oil or parchment paper; if not, the breading will stick.

Once all of the chicken is coated, drizzle a little olive oil over each chicken breast and bake them in the oven for 18–22 minutes or until the centers are no longer pink (depending on how thick the chicken breasts are). Then turn up the heat and broil for 5 minutes or until the breading is golden brown.

Serves 4

SHRIMP, CHICKEN, AND ANDOUILLE SAUSAGE JAMBALAYA

1 Tbsp Olive Oil	½ Green Bell Pepper	½ tsp Cayenne Powder
1 Chicken Breast	1½ ribs Celery	½ tsp Oregano
12 Jumbo Shrimp	3 cloves Garlic	½ tsp Thyme
2 Andouille Sausages	1 head Cauliflower	1 cup Chicken Stock
Adobo Seasoning	2 Bay Leaves	¾ cup Water
(see page 14)	1 ½ tsp Sea Salt	½ Tbsp Honey
Creole Seasoning	1 tsp Black Pepper	1 Beefsteak Tomato
1 Small Yellow Onion	½ tsp Paprika	2 Tbsp Parsley
½ Red Bell Pepper	½ tsp Ground Chipotle Pepper	

Dice the chicken and peel the shrimp. Dust both lightly with Adobo Seasoning and creole spices. Keep the shrimp and chicken separate and set aside.

Dice the onion, peppers, celery, and garlic. Slice the sausages into ¼" pieces. Heat the oil in a large pan over medium-high heat and sauté the diced ingredients for 4–6 minutes, or until the onions are translucent.

Next, rice the cauliflower by food-processing or finely chopping. Add the cauliflower, diced chicken, black pepper, sea salt, paprika, chipotle pepper, cayenne, oregano, and thyme to the onion mixture. Cook for 2–3 minutes.

Add the chicken stock, water, diced tomatoes, bay leaves, and honey to the onion mixture and bring to a boil.

Cover and reduce the heat to medium-low (~3) and simmer for 20 minutes, stirring occasionally.

Lastly, add the shrimp and cook another 4–6 minutes, or until the shrimp is pink and cooked through. Let stand for about 5 minutes, remove the bay leaves from the jambalaya, stir in the parsley, and serve.

Serves 4 to 6

WILD CAUGHT

Coconut-Crusted Cod • Lemon Dill Salmon • Blackened Salmon
Salmon and Sautéed Onions over Sweet Potato Mash • Ahi Tuna Tartare
Coconut-Crusted Shrimp • Bang Bang Shrimp • Curried Scallops with Spinach
Thai Mixed Vegetables • Seafood Medley with Tomato Sauce

COCONUT-CRUSTED COD

4 Cod Fillets	½ tsp Madras Yellow Curry Powder	1 tsp Sea Salt
⅔ cup Coconut Flour		1 tsp Black Pepper
1 Tbsp Adobo Seasoning (see page 14)	½ tsp Cumin	1 Egg
	¼ Ground Coriander	1 cup Coconut Milk
1 cup Unsweetened Coconut Flakes	1 tsp Coconut Crystals	3 Tbsp Coconut Oil

Grease a pan big enough for all fillets with coconut oil.

Next, set up 3 bowls, making sure to mix each bowl thoroughly to combine the ingredients.

In bowl 1, combine the coconut flour and Adobo Seasoning. In bowl 2, combine the coconut milk and egg. And in bowl 3, combine the coconut flakes, yellow curry, cumin, coriander, coconut crystals, sea salt, and black pepper.

Heat the coconut oil over medium-high heat (~6.5). While the oil is heating, prepare the fish.

Take one cod fillet and make an assembly line: first, coat in bowl 1, then dunk into bowl 2, and lastly, coat in bowl 3. Repeat with all fish fillets until all fish are coated.

Once the oil is hot (do a drip test: drop a tiny speck of coconut flake into the oil; if it starts to bubble, we're good to go), add the fish to the pan.

Sauté each fish for about 3–4 minutes on each side, depending on how thick the fish is. If you know your fish is really thick, turn the pan heat down to medium (~4), as you don't want your coconut crust to burn.

Serves 4

This recipe is Pescatarian

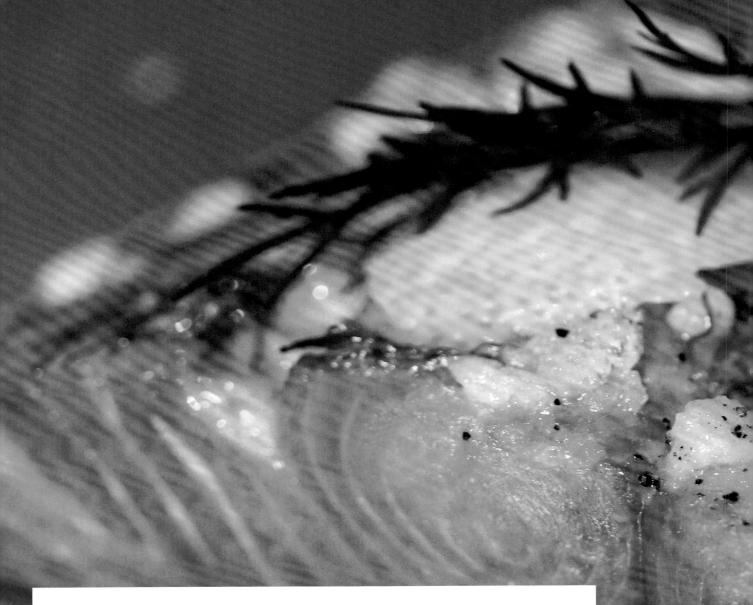

LEMON DILL SALMON

4 Sockeye Salmon
fillets (with skin)

Juice of 1 Lemon

½ tsp Lemon Zest

2 Tbsp Olive Oil

1 tsp Dill

2 cloves Garlic
(minced)

Sea Salt

Put all ingredients except for the sea salt in a ziplock bag and marinate for at least 20 minutes (we prefer 1–2 hours if we have the time).

Preheat the oven to 375 degrees Fahrenheit.

Take the salmon out of the bag and place on an ungreased grill pan or baking sheet, skin side down, and dust the top with sea salt. The key here is ungreased, so that the skin will stick to the pan and the fish will slide right off. If you want to serve your salmon with the skins on, then grease the baking sheet.

Cook the salmon in the middle rack of the oven for 22–25 minutes.

Serves 4

This recipe is Pescatarian

BLACKENED SALMON

4 Sockeye Salmon fillets (with skin)	Creole Seasoning OR	1 Tbsp Oregano
	1 Tbsp Paprika	1 Tbsp Sea Salt
Olive Oil	1 Tbsp Cayenne Powder	1 Tbsp Black Pepper
	1 Tbsp Thyme	

Mix the spices together and spread out on a plate.

Rub the flesh side of the salmon with a little olive oil and press the fillets (flesh side down) onto the spices, making sure that they are covered with spice.

Heat 2–3 tablespoons of oil in a pan over medium heat. Once it is hot, turn off the burner.

Place the fillets, flesh side down, in the pan, in one layer, so they all have contact with the pan. Then turn the heat back on medium (~4) and cook for 2 minutes.

After 2 minutes, turn the heat down to medium-low (~2) and flip the salmon (using tongs is easiest). The spiced, flesh side should be crispy and the skin should be in contact with the pan.

Cover and cook at low (~2) for another 12–16 minutes, skin should be crispy at this point. If you are unsure how long to cook your fish, it should equal about 8 minutes per 1 inch of thickness in the meat (or 145 degrees Fahrenheit at the thickest part).

Serves 4

This recipe is Pescatarian

SALMON & SAUTÉED ONIONS OVER SWEET POTATO MASH

4 Sockeye Salmon fillets (with skin)	Sea Salt	¾ cup Coconut Milk
3 Sweet Potatoes	1 Tbsp Adobo Seasoning (see page 14)	¼ cup Coconut Crystals
1 White Onion	¾ cup Coconut Oil	¾ cup White Wine (or Water)
		Black Pepper (to taste)

Preheat the oven to 275 degrees Fahrenheit.

Boil a large pot of water with a ½ Tbsp sea salt.

Dust the salmon with sea salt on all sides. Bake skin side down on a baking sheet or grill pan for 15–20 minutes.

While the fish is baking, peel the sweet potatoes, cut them in thirds, add them to the boiling water, and cook, uncovered, for 15–20 minutes.

While the fish and potatoes are cooking, heat the coconut oil in a pan over medium heat (~5). Julienne the white onion and add it to the hot oil. While the onions are lightly sizzling add the Adobo Seasoning and the white wine (or water).

Season with black pepper to taste. Leave covered for 15 minutes, then reduce the temperature to low and let sit for an additional 5 minutes.

Once the sweet potatoes are done cooking (they will be soft when poked with a fork), remove them from the water and place in a bowl. Add the coconut milk and coconut crystals. Mash well.

On the serving plate, layer some mashed sweet potato first, then place a salmon fillet and top with the sautéed onions (before serving the onions, turn the heat up to high, sizzle briefly, then top the dish).

Serves 4

This recipe is Pescatarian

AHI TUNA TARTARE

4 Sashimi Grade Ahi Tuna Fillets	*Sesame Poke Sauce:*	6 cloves Garlic
3 Avocados	8 Tbsp Coconut Aminos (or Wheat-Free Tamari)	8 tsp Coconut Crystals (or Honey)
Sea Salt	4 Tbsp Sesame Oil	8 Arbol Chili Peppers
	2 Tbsp Coconut Vinegar	½ tsp Ginger

First, make the sauce by combining all Sesame Poke Sauce ingredients in a blender.

Slice strips of both the tuna and avocado. Sprinkle with a little sea salt, then cover with the poke sauce. It is easiest to arrange on a springform pan, but you can serve this in a bowl or dish as well.

Tip Make sure that the tuna that you get is sashimi grade. As there is no cooking involved in this recipe, we want to buy fish that is meant to be eaten raw. If you are unsure, we suggest heating coconut oil or sesame oil over high heat, and *very* quickly searing on each side.

Serves 4

This recipe is Pescatarian

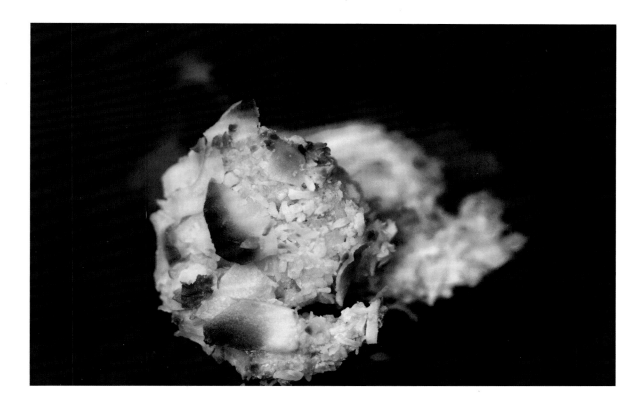

COCONUT-CRUSTED SHRIMP

15-20 Jumbo Shrimp	¼ tsp Cayenne Powder	2 cups Coconut Flakes (unsweetened)
⅓ cup Almond Flour	1 Egg White	
½ tsp Sea Salt	1 Tbsp Coconut Milk	

Preheat the oven to 400 degrees Fahrenheit.

Lay the shrimp out on a paper towel and pat dry.

In bowl 1, combine the almond flour, sea salt, and cayenne. In bowl 2, whip the egg white and coconut milk until fluffy. In bowl 3, place the coconut flakes.

Coat the shrimp in the flour mixture, then the egg, then the coconut flakes, and place on a baking sheet lined with parchment paper (or greased if you don't have any).

Cook on the middle rack of the oven for 12–15 minutes.

Tip Serve with our Shrimp Sauce (see page 50)!

Serves 2 to 4

This recipe is Pescatarian

BANG BANG SHRIMP

Fried Shrimp:

15-20 Jumbo Shrimp

2 Eggs

2 Tbsp Arrowroot
    Powder

Breading:

1 tsp Arrowroot Powder

½ cup Almond Flour

½ cup Coconut Flakes
    (unsweetened)

¼ tsp Onion Powder

¼ tsp Garlic Powder

¼ tsp Adobo Seasoning
    (see page 14)

¼ tsp Sea Salt

¼ tsp Black Pepper

Coconut Oil

Bang Bang Sauce:

¼ cup Mayonnaise
    (see page 14)

4 Tbsp Sweet Chili Sauce
    (see page 18)

1 tsp Coconut Vinegar

Garnish:

2 Green Onions

Shredded Cabbage

Combine the breading ingredients in a bowl and set aside.

Next, we'll prepare the fried shrimp. Beat the 2 eggs lightly, then mix in the arrowroot powder. Once thoroughly incorporated, add the de-shelled, de-tailed, de-veined shrimp.

Coat the shrimp in the egg mixture, then cover with breading, then place on a baking sheet lined with parchment paper (or greased if you don't have any). Shape them the way you want them to cook.

If you are not using parchment paper, once the shrimp have all been breaded, put the baking sheet in the refrigerator for at least 30 minutes. This will help the breading stick to the shrimp. Sometimes, we do this even a couple hours in advance. If you are using parchment paper, you don't need to do this at all.

For Frying: Heat the coconut oil in a pan over medium-high (~6) heat. Always do a test to make sure that the oil is hot enough: a piece of coconut flake or breading should sizzle when dropped into the oil.

Fry the shrimp in the oil until each side is golden brown. This should take about 3–4 minutes on each side. If they are turning brown too quickly, turn down the heat a little.

When golden brown, remove from the oil and drain on a paper towel.

For Oven Baking: Bake at 400 degrees Fahrenheit for 16–18 minutes or until golden brown.

Once cooked, toss the shrimp in the bang bang sauce until adequately coated.

Chop the green onions. Lay down a layer of either shredded cabbage or wilted spinach, and then the shrimp. Then top with the green onions and serve!

Serves 2 to 4

This recipe is Pescatarian

CURRIED SCALLOPS WITH SPINACH

1 lb Scallops

1 cup Baby Spinach

1 Tbsp Coconut Oil

½ cup Sweet Onion

2 cloves Garlic

1 tsp Ginger

2 tsp Madras Yellow
   Curry Powder

½ tsp Cumin

½ tsp Coriander

1 cup Coconut Milk

⅔ cup Chicken Stock

1 tsp Sea Salt

Heat the coconut oil over medium-high heat (~7). Add the diced onions to the oil and cook for about 2 minutes, or until they begin to turn translucent. Turn the heat down to medium (~5) and add the garlic and ginger and stir until fragrant, about 1 minute.

Once fragrant, turn the heat down again (~4) and add the Madras yellow curry, cumin, and coriander and stir to incorporate. Then add the coconut milk, chicken stock, and sliced baby spinach (sans the stems) and stir to incorporate. Season the mixture with sea salt, to taste.

Once all ingredients are incorporated, add the scallops gently. You do not want them to fall apart. Spoon a little of the juices over the scallops, cover partially, and cook about 4–6 minutes, until they are slightly bouncy to the touch (push your finger into the middle of the scallop, and when you let go, it should bounce back a little—not a lot, but a little).

Once bouncy, take them off the heat and serve with the liquids and spinach.

Tip You can use any type of scallops, but we prefer sea scallops.

Serves 2 to 4

This recipe can easily be made Pescatarian, just swap the chicken stock for vegetable.

THAI MIXED VEGETABLES

5 Tbsp Coconut Aminos

4 Tbsp Chicken Stock

2 Tbsp Roasted Red Chili Paste

2 Tbsp Ginger

4 Arbol Chili Peppers

1 ½ Tbsp Honey

2 tsp Fish Sauce

2 tsp Coconut Vinegar

2 tsp Sesame Oil

½ Tbsp Arrowroot Powder

2 Tbsp Coconut Oil

2 cups Broccoli florets

6 Baby Portobello Mushrooms

1 Red Bell Pepper

½ Yellow Onion

2 Carrots

½ Zucchini

½ Japanese Eggplant

Optional: Shrimp (or other protein)

Prep the vegetables by removing the stems and seeds, cutting everything into bite-sized chunks, and then set aside.

Combine the coconut aminos, chicken stock, red chili paste, ginger, arbol chilies, coconut crystals, fish sauce, coconut vinegar, sesame oil, and arrowroot powder and blend until smooth. Set aside.

Heat the coconut oil in a large pan or wok over medium-high heat (~7). Add the broccoli and carrots, making sure to coat them all in the oil, then cook, covered, for about 2 minutes. Add the remaining vegetables, cover, and cook for another 3–5 minutes, stirring frequently.

When the broccoli is bright green and the onions are starting to turn translucent, add the shrimp. Stir to incorporate. After about a minute or two, add the sauce.

Stir the vegetables frequently, over medium-low heat (~3), until the sauce is thick and the shrimp is heated through.

Tip If you are not using leftover meat, cut the raw meat into chunks, heat 1 tablespoon oil over medium-high heat, cook until no longer pink, and set aside. You will want to do this first.

Serves 4

This recipe can easily be made Pescatarian, just swap the chicken stock with vegetable.

SEAFOOD MEDLEY WITH TOMATO SAUCE

1 lb Seafood*	¼ cup Coconut Milk	1 ½ Tbsp Capers
Adobo Seasoning (see page 14)	4 Tbsp Olive Oil	1 ½ cups Baby Spinach
	½ cup Parsley	8 Baby Portobello Mushrooms
8 cloves Garlic	1 ½ Tbsp White Wine (or Chicken Stock)	
1 cup Sweet Onion		Sea Salt and Black Pepper (to taste)
1 cup Diced Tomatoes	1 ½ Tbsp Lemon Juice	

*We like a variety of seafood, including shrimp, mussels, octopus, calamari, and fish.

Dice the onions. Heat the oil over medium-high heat (~7). Once hot, add the onions and cook, stirring, until lightly browned and caramelized. Then turn the heat a little lower (~5), add the garlic, and cook for another minute, stirring, until the garlic is fragrant. You do not want this to burn or it will taste bitter.

Next, dust the seafood in Adobo Seasoning. Add to the pot, stir, cover, and cook for about 3 minutes.

While the seafood is cooking, slice the baby spinach (we remove the stems) into strips and halve the mushrooms.

Add the spinach, mushrooms, and all remaining ingredients (reserving just a little parsley for garnish) to the pot and cook, covered, until the mussels open and the shrimp is pink and cooked throughout. You will want to stir occasionally and spice with sea salt and black pepper appropriately.

Serves 4

This recipe is Pescatarian

SWEETS

Chewy Chocolate Chip Cookies • N-Oatmeal Raisin Cookies • Coconut Macaroons • Brownies
Chocolate Frosting • Chocolate Cake • Banana Bread • Fried Sweet Plantains with Vanilla Bean Ice Cream
Tropical Avocado Popsicles • Piña Colada Ice Cream • Peach Ice Cream • Strawberry Ice Cream
Banana Soufflé • Baked Apple Pie • Pecan Pie • Pumpkin Pie • Lemon Vanilla Crème Brûlée
Lemon Flan • Maple-Glazed Pear Cheesecake • Honey Mango Meringue Pie

CHEWY CHOCOLATE CHIP COOKIES

¾ cup Almond Flour	¼ tsp Sea Salt	1 Tbsp Vanilla Extract
¼ cup Golden Flaxseed Meal	½ tsp Baking Soda	3 drops Almond Extract
¼ cup Coconut Flour	3 oz Dark Chocolate Chips (enjoy life)	½ cup Coconut Oil
2 Tbsp Arrowroot Powder	1 Tbsp Honey	½ tsp Walnut Oil
		1 Egg

Preheat the oven to 350 degree Fahrenheit.

In a bowl, mix the almond flour, coconut flour, flaxseed meal, baking soda, arrowroot powder, and dark chocolate.

Combine the honey, vanilla extract, almond extract, coconut oil, walnut oil, sea salt, and egg and blend until thoroughly incorporated.

Mix the wet ingredients into the dry. Line a cookie sheet with parchment paper (or grease with oil if you don't have any parchment paper).

Take a spoonful of dough and drop it onto the baking sheet. It should be 2" to 3" across and about ¼" thick. It is important to note that however they look on the pan is how they will look when they are done. So if they are ugly going in, they will be ugly coming out.

Cook in the oven on the middle rack for 9–12 minutes, depending on the thickness of your cookies.

Makes 18 to 20

This recipe is Vegetarian

N-OATMEAL RAISIN COOKIES

1 ½ cups Almond Flour	1 tsp Baking Soda	1 Vanilla Bean
¼ cup Golden Flaxseed Meal	½ cup Coconut Milk	½ tsp Cinnamon
¼ cup Coconut Flour	3 Tbsp Maple Syrup	½ tsp Sea Salt
¼ cup Coconut Flakes (unsweetened)	1 Tbsp Coconut Oil	1 cup Raisins
	1 Egg	

Cut the vanilla bean lengthwise, then scrape out the insides with the back side of a knife; you want only the insides.

Preheat the oven to 325 degrees Fahrenheit. Line a baking sheet with parchment paper (or grease the baking sheet if you don't have any parchment paper) and set aside for later.

In a bowl, combine the almond flour, flaxseed meal, coconut flour, coconut flakes, baking soda, and raisins. Mix to incorporate.

In a separate bowl, combine the coconut milk, maple syrup, coconut oil, egg, vanilla bean, cinnamon, and sea salt. You will want to mix these until thoroughly blended.

Add the wet to the dry, and mix. Once all ingredients are incorporated, spoon out about 2 tablespoons of batter per cookie and drop them onto the baking sheet.

Bake the cookies for 15–20 minutes, or until a toothpick comes out clean and the cookies are slightly browned on the top.

Makes 20 to 22

This recipe is Vegetarian

COCONUT MACAROONS

2 Egg Whites	½ tsp Almond Extract	2 tsp Arrowroot Powder
2 Tbsp Honey	1 ½ cups Coconut Flakes (unsweetened)	pinch Sea Salt
½ tsp Vanilla Extract		

Preheat the oven to 350 degrees Fahrenheit.

Whip the egg whites until they are fluffy, but not stiff. I use a hand mixer and it only takes a couple of minutes, but if you don't have one, use a whisk and hang in there, as it will take a few minutes.

Mix the honey, vanilla extract, almond extract, coconut flakes, arrowroot powder, and sea salt in a bowl, then add the mix to the eggs. Careful! You want to fold them in and try not to overdo it. The more you mix the eggs, the less fluffy they will be when they are cooked.

Then line a baking sheet with parchment paper. It will make removing the cookies simple and clean. If you don't have parchment paper, you'll want to lightly grease the baking sheet.

Once you have the baking sheet lined, drop about a tablespoon of the mixture onto the sheet. Space your macaroons 1" to 2" apart.

Bake on the middle rack for 12–15 minutes. You will see that the tops will brown and a toothpick will come out clean.

Makes 10

This recipe is Vegetarián

BROWNIES

½ cup Almond Flour   1 Tbsp Coconut Milk   ½ Tbsp Brandy (if you drink brandy, if not, omit)

½ cup Cocoa Powder   2 Eggs

2 Tbsp Coconut Flour   ⅓ cup Honey   ½ cup Coconut Oil

¼ tsp Sea Salt   ⅔ cup Coconut Crystals   *Optional:* 3 oz Dark Chocolate (enjoy life)

¼ tsp Baking Soda   1 Tbsp Vanilla Extract

Preheat the oven to 350 degrees Fahrenheit and grease an 8" × 8" baking dish or 2 large ramekins (as pictured).

In a bowl, combine the almond flour, cocoa powder, coconut flour, sea salt, and baking soda. Set aside for later.

Blend the eggs, honey, coconut crystals, vanilla, coconut milk, and brandy (if you are using this). Set aside for later.

If you are using the chocolate, heat the coconut oil on low (~4) and once warm, remove from the heat and add the chocolate. We use sea-salted dark chocolate and omit the ¼ teaspoon sea salt. It will melt the chunks within a minute, so keep on stirring.

Pour the chocolate and oil into the dry ingredients. Mix to take the temperature of the oil down, then slowly add the egg mixture while whisking.

If you aren't using the chocolate, combine the wet ingredients and sugar in a blender and add to dry ingredients.

Pour the mixture into the greased 8" × 8" baking dish (or ramekins). We use coconut oil, but any will do. Bake for 32–35 minutes.

Tip You can get away with using only one kind of flour and sugar, but it does actually make a difference in the way these taste. Not a big deal if you want to simplify, but this is our recommendation.

This recipe is Vegetarian

CHOCOLATE CAKE

⅓ cup Ground Cashews (unsalted)	5 Eggs	½ cup Coconut Oil
¼ cup Cocoa Powder	½ cup Honey	½ tsp Sea Salt
	1 Tbsp Vanilla Extract	½ tsp Baking Soda

Preheat the oven to 350 degrees Fahrenheit.

Mix everything together in a blender until the ingredients are incorporated.

Transfer the batter into an 8", baking dish or into individual ramekins that have been greased with coconut oil and a little cocoa powder.

Bake for 32–35 minutes, covered, or until a toothpick comes out clean.

This recipe is Vegetarian

CHOCOLATE FROSTING

½ cup Coconut Oil	1 tsp Vanilla Extract	4 Tbsp Coconut Milk
¼ cup Honey	¾ cup Cocoa Powder	pinch Sea Salt

Mix everything except the sea salt together in a blender until the ingredients are smooth and incorporated. We like to spoon the frosting into a bag or cake decorator.

Spread it over or decorate your chocolate cake and sprinkle with a little sea salt.

Tip We use the coconut milk in a can, full fat—it sets up better than the liquid kind.

This recipe is Vegan

BANANA BREAD

2 Very Ripe Bananas

¼ cup Honey

¼ cup Applesauce

1 Tbsp Coconut Oil

1 tsp Vanilla Extract

2 Eggs

1 cup Almond Flour

⅓ cup Golden Flaxseed Meal

⅓ cup Coconut Flour

1 tsp Lemon Juice

1 tsp Baking Soda

½ tsp Cinnamon

pinch of Sea Salt

Optional: ½ cup Blueberries

Optional: Walnuts or Almonds (to top)

Preheat the oven to 325 degrees Fahrenheit.

Mash the bananas, then add the honey, applesauce, coconut oil, vanilla extract, and lemon juice. Whisk in the eggs.

Sift in the dry ingredients and blueberries if you are using them. Fold the dry into the wet until incorporated.

Bake in a greased loaf pan (ours is metal, about 9" x 5") for 1 hour. Watch it. At around 45 minutes, you may need to cover it with tin foil to keep the top from getting too dark.

Makes 1 loaf

This recipe is Vegetarian

FRIED SWEET PLANTAINS WITH
VANILLA BEAN ICE CREAM

Plantains:

2 Plantains

Coconut Oil

Vanilla Bean Ice Cream:

14 oz Coconut Milk

2 Eggs

2 Tbsp Honey

3 Vanilla Beans

⅛ tsp Meyer Lemon Juice

pinch Sea Salt

Put the coconut milk on the stove and heat to medium-high. Scrape the insides of the vanilla bean out with the back of a knife and add to the coconut milk. Heat, whisking, until the vanilla bean is evenly distributed and the oils begin to break out of the coconut milk. Take off the heat.

Mix the eggs to incorporate and then slowly whisk them into the milk mixture. The key is to add the eggs very slowly and constantly whisk. You don't want them to cook in the coconut milk.

Then add the sea salt, honey, and lemon juice.

Cool the mixture to room temperature. Once cool, add it to the ice cream maker and follow the instructions on your ice cream machine (ours instructs to layer the ice and the rock salt and let it go for 20 minutes).

If you don't have an ice cream maker, you can put the mixture in the freezer and stir every 10-15 minutes until it is the consistency you want. It won't be quite the same, but it will suffice.

As the ice cream is churning in the ice cream maker, peel and cut the sweet plantains into 3" pieces. Heat the coconut oil in a pot over high heat (~8). Do a drop test by dropping a small piece of plantain into the oil. If it sizzles, the oil is hot and ready. Fry the plantains until golden brown and warmed through-out. Serve with our Vanilla Bean Ice Cream.

Tip The plantains need to be black. Not green, not yellow, but black. If they are not black, this recipe will not turn out. If you have green plantains, place them somewhere dark and let them turn black.

Tip We use full-fat coconut milk.

Tip This ice cream is best when made fresh.

Serves 4

This recipe is Vegetarian but can be made Vegan if you omit the eggs

TROPICAL AVOCADO POPSICLES

1 Avocado	½ cup Coconut Milk	1 Tbsp Lime Juice
1 Kiwi	2 Tbsp Honey	pinch Sea Salt

Scrape the avocado pulp into a food processor or blender and add the honey, coconut milk, lime juice, and sea salt.

Cut the kiwi in half and scrape the seeds into a separate bowl. Once removed, add the green kiwi pulp to the food processor or blender. You want to remove the seeds before you blend everything because they have a tendency to taste bitter if not whole.

If you want to add the seeds into the mixture after it is blended, do it now and mix them in.

Spoon the mixture into popsicle molds and freeze until set.

Makes 4

This recipe is Vegan

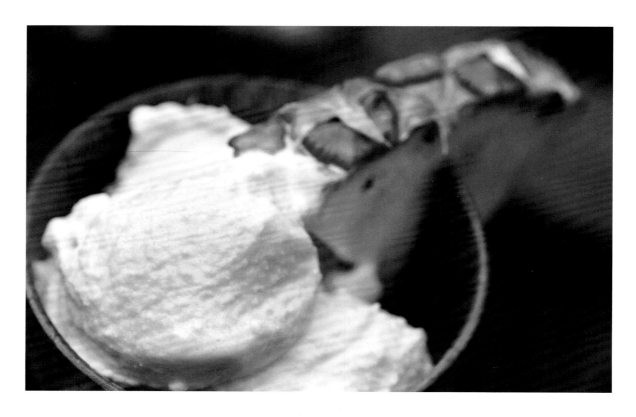

PEACH ICE CREAM

3 Peaches

14 oz Coconut Milk

¼ cup Honey

1 tsp Lemon Juice

½ tsp Sea Salt

Optional: ⅛ tsp Almond Extract

Optional: 2 Basil or Mint Leaves

Optional: Toasted Almond Slices

Peel and pit the peaches. Smash the peaches and add them directly into the ice cream maker.

Add the coconut milk, honey, lemon juice, sea salt, and almond extract to a blender and blend until smooth. Add the mixture to the peaches.

If you are going to use the optional ingredients, mince the basil/mint and toasted almonds first, then add them to the peaches and coconut milk.

Follow the instructions on your ice cream machine (ours instructs to layer the ice and the rock salt and let it go for 20 minutes).

If you don't have an ice cream maker, you can put the mixture in the freezer and stir every 10–15 minutes until it is the consistency you want. It won't be quite the same, but it will suffice.

Tip We use full-fat coconut milk.

Tip This ice cream is best when made fresh.

Serves 4

This recipe is Vegan

PIÑA COLADA ICE CREAM

14 oz Coconut Milk

1 cup Pineapple Juice

½ cup Orange Juice

2 cups Pineapple

4 Egg Yolks

pinch Sea Salt

Put the coconut milk on the stove and heat to medium (~5). Heat until the oils begin to break out of the cream. Take off the heat.

Mix the eggs to incorporate and then slowly whisk them into the milk mixture. The key is to add the eggs very slowly and constantly whisk. You don't want them to cook in the milk. This is called tempering the eggs.

Then add the sea salt, orange juice, and pineapple juice.

Blend the pineapple in a food processor or blender and then add it to the milk mixture.

Let the mixture cool to room temperature. Once cool, add it to the ice cream maker and follow the instructions on your ice cream machine (ours instructs to layer the ice and the rock salt and let it go for 20 minutes).

If you don't have an ice cream maker, you can put the mixture in the freezer and stir every 10–15 minutes until it is the consistency you want.

Tip We use full-fat coconut milk.

Tip This ice cream is best when made fresh.

Serves 4

This recipe is Vegetarian but can be made Vegan if you omit the egg yolks

STRAWBERRY ICE CREAM

14 oz Coconut Milk	2 Tbsp Honey	1 cup Very Ripe Strawberries
1 Vanilla Bean	1 tsp Meyer Lemon Juice	
2 Eggs		pinch Sea Salt

Put the coconut milk on the stove and heat to medium-high. Scrape the insides of the vanilla bean out with the back of a knife and add to the coconut milk. Heat, whisking, until the vanilla bean is evenly distributed and the oils begin to break out of the coconut milk. Take off the heat.

Mix the eggs to incorporate and then slowly whisk them into the milk mixture. The key is to add the eggs very slowly and constantly whisk. You don't want them to cook in the coconut milk.

Then add the sea salt, honey, and lemon juice.

Hull the strawberries, then blend them in a food processor or blender. Add them to the coconut milk mixture.

Let the mixture cool to room temperature. Once cool, add it to the ice cream maker and follow the instructions on your ice cream machine (ours instructs to layer the ice and the rock salt and let it go for 20 minutes).

If you don't have an ice cream maker, you can put the mixture in the freezer and stir every 10-15 minutes until it is the consistency you want. It won't be quite the same, but it will suffice.

Tip We use full-fat coconut milk.

Tip This ice cream is best when made fresh.

Serves 4

This recipe is Vegetarian but can be made Vegan if you omit the eggs

BANANA SOUFFLÉ

2 Ripe Bananas	⅓ cup + 1 Tbsp Coconut Crystals	pinch Cinnamon
1 Tbsp Arrowroot Powder		pinch Sea Salt
3 Tbsp Water	4 Egg Whites	Coconut Oil

Preheat the oven to 400 degrees Fahrenheit.

Oil 4 (4 oz) ramekins and set aside.

Peel and puree the bananas. The riper they are, the easier they will be to smash.

Boil the water and coconut crystals. Then add the bananas to the water and coconut crystals mixture and stir. Then add the arrowroot powder and cinnamon. Cook until the coconut crystals have dissolved.

Once the coconut crystals have dissolved, take off the stove and allow the mixture to cool down completely. It will look chunky and odd, but this is correct.

In a stainless-steel bowl, whip the eggs and sea salt until they are frothy. Then add 1 tablespoon of coconut crystals and continue to whip until the eggs have stiff peaks. This is important. They must be *stiff* peaks.

Fold the banana mixture into the eggs. Then pour into the ramekins.

Place the ramekins on a baking sheet. Place in the oven, then immediately turn the heat down to 375 degrees Fahrenheit.

Bake for 10–12 minutes or until golden brown. Serve immediately.

Serves 4

This recipe is Vegetarian

BAKED APPLE PIE

Preheat the oven to 350 degrees Fahrenheit.

For the Crust: Food-process the crust ingredients. If you don't have a food processor, then crush the nuts, mince the dates, and combine all with the remaining crust ingredients.

Press the crust mixture into a greased (with coconut oil) 8" or 9" springform pan, or 3 individual 3" pie pans. We like to use a spring-form pan because it makes removing the pie easier, but it isn't imperative. Poke the crust with a fork several times and bake, uncovered, for 12–15 minutes. Watch it at the end, so it doesn't burn. Remove the crust from the heat, and once cool enough, gently press down on the bottom part of the crust, so it really sticks together nicely as it cools.

For the Filling: While the crust is baking and cooling, peel the apples, de-core them, and dice them. Put the apples and apple juice in a pan and bring to a boil. Reduce the heat to medium-low (~4) and simmer for 5 minutes.

Next, mix together the arrowroot powder and water to make a slurry. Cut the vanilla bean pods lengthwise into 2 halves. Use the blunt edge of a knife to scrape out the insides, then add it to the slurry. Add this, along with the maple syrup, lemon juice, sea salt, cinnamon, and nutmeg, to the apples.

Cook, stirring, until the juices begin to thicken. This should take about 2 minutes. Then pour the warm apple mixture into the finished, pressed nut crust.

Bake, uncovered, for 15–20 minutes (for 3" pies) or 30–35 minutes (for 8" to 9" pie), or until the apples are bubbling and the center is hot.

Tip This is perfect with our Vanilla Bean Ice Cream! (see page 180)

Makes 8" pie

This recipe is Vegan

PECAN PIE

Crust:	3 Egg Whites	¼ cup Coconut Crystals
½ cup Coconut Flour	Coconut Oil	2 Tbsp Arrowroot
½ cup Coconut Flakes		Powder + 2 Tbsp Water
(unsweetened)	Filling:	(= slurry)
½ Tbsp Maple Syrup	1 Egg White	¼ tsp Sea Salt
¼ tsp Sea Salt	1 Egg	¼ tsp Vanilla Extract
¼ cup Coconut Oil	1 cup Maple Syrup	6 oz Pecan Halves

For the crust: Preheat the oven to 400 degrees Fahrenheit.

Mix the maple syrup, sea salt, coconut oil, and egg whites. Sift in the coconut flour and coconut flakes. Mix until incorporated. Grease a pie pan or springform pie pan (which will make the pie easier to remove) with coconut oil and press the dough into the pan. Press it into the pan thinly and evenly. Poke the bottom of the crust a couple of times with a fork and bake, uncovered, for 10 minutes.

For the Filling: Combine the egg white, egg, maple syrup, coconut crystals, slurry, sea salt, and vanilla and blend until thoroughly incorporated. Pour the pecans into the pie crust, then top with the egg mixture. Wrap the edges of the pie crust in tin foil to prevent burning. Bake for 40 minutes uncovered or until set.

Tip For more Thanksgiving Day recipes, visit our blog at www.paleoeffect.com!

Makes 8" pie

This recipe is Vegetarian

PUMPKIN PIE

Crust:

½ cup Coconut Flour

½ cup Coconut Flakes
  (unsweetened)

½ Tbsp Maple Syrup

¼ tsp Sea Salt

· ¼ cup Coconut Oil

3 Egg Whites

Coconut Oil

Filling:

2 Eggs

¼ cup Maple Syrup

¼ tsp Ground Ginger

¼ tsp Allspice

¼ tsp Sea Salt

pinch of Cinnamon

1 ¾ cups Pumpkin Puree

1 cup Coconut Milk

For the Crust: Preheat the oven to 400 degrees Fahrenheit.

Mix the maple syrup, sea salt, coconut oil, and egg whites. Sift in the coconut flour and coconut flakes. Mix until incorporated. Grease a pie pan or springform pie pan (which will make the pie easier to remove) with coconut oil and press the dough into the pan. Press it into the pan thinly and evenly. Poke the bottom of the crust a couple of times with a fork and bake, uncovered, for 10 minutes.

For the Filling: Increase the oven temperature to 450 degrees Fahrenheit.

Whip the eggs, then add the maple syrup. Add the spices and mix until blended. Next, add the coconut milk and pumpkin puree. Pour mixture into the pie crust. Wrap the edges of the pie crust in tin foil to prevent burning. Cook for 12 minutes, then turn the heat down to 350 degrees Fahrenheit and cook for another 30 minutes, or until a toothpick comes out clean.

Tip This recipe tastes great with our Vanilla Bean Ice Cream! (see page 180)

Makes 8" pie

This recipe is Vegetarian

LEMON VANILLA CRÈME BRÛLÉE

6 Egg Yolks	1 ½ cups Coconut Milk	1 Vanilla Bean
2 ½ tsp Lemon Zest	6 Tbsp Honey	Coconut Oil

Preheat the oven to 350 degrees Fahrenheit.

Let the eggs come to room temperature. Whip them in a bowl until they are slightly thickened.

Add the honey, and mix into the egg yolks. Cut the vanilla bean in half, scrape the seeds out with the blunt edge of a knife, and add to the egg mixture. Then add the lemon zest and coconut milk and incorporate. Let stand for 10–15 minutes, then strain it (so you don't get a mouthful of lemon zest).

Set 4 ramekins in a glass dish and fill the glass halfway with hot water. Grease the ramekins with coconut oil and then pour the egg mixture into the ramekins.

Place the dish in the oven on the middle rack and bake for 30–40 minutes, turning once so that the custard cooks evenly. You will know when they are done because the custard will look thick when you wiggle the dish. It should not look like liquid. If it does, leave it in longer. The top will be slightly browned and it will jiggle when you wiggle it.

Serves 4

This recipe is Vegetarian

LEMON FLAN

| 1 cup Coconut Crystals | 1 can Coconut Milk | Rind of 1 Lemon |
| 4 Large Eggs | 1 Vanilla Bean | pinch Sea Salt |

Preheat the oven to 350 degrees Fahrenheit.

Take a ½ cup coconut crystals and put a thin layer in the bottom of each ramekin. If you are using sugarcane instead, put it in a saucepan and heat it slowly until all the sugar melts, stirring frequently. Then pour it into 6 (6-ounce) ramekins.

Next, beat the eggs until smooth. Set them aside.

Cut the yellow part of the rind off of the lemon. If you get a little white, that is perfectly OK. Then cut the rind into thinner strips—this is not rocket science. It does not matter what they look like; you just want to cut them down so the oils can get out. Then put them in a saucepan.

In the same saucepan, bring the coconut milk, remaining ½ cup coconut crystals (or sugarcane), vanilla bean (cut lengthwise, then scrape out the insides with the blunt edge of a knife), sea salt, and lemon rind to a boil. Once it starts to bubble, turn down the heat, cover with a lid, and let simmer for 5 minutes. After 5 minutes, take the mixture and strain it into a separate bowl to remove all of the lemon rinds. Let it sit for 5 minutes (or more if you like; this is just to cool it down a little).

With a whisk in one hand and the eggs in another, slowly add the eggs to the milk mixture, whisking constantly. Pour slowly over the coconut crystals, taking care not to let the coconut crystals disperse into the milk mixture. The goal here is to have a sweet caramel-like topping when you flip it out of the ramekin. If you used sugar, it will be hard at this point — really hard, like a rock — so you won't have any issues with pouring.

Next, you want to take a baking dish, place the ramekins in it, then fill around them with warm water until the dish is ⅔ full.

Bake 40–45 minutes. When done, the top of the flan will look a little tan and will be a little set. If you wiggle the pan, the flan will be a very thick liquid.

Take them out of the dish and put them in the refrigerator for at least a couple of hours, or overnight if you have the time.

Serves 4

This recipe is Vegetarian

MAPLE-GLAZED PEAR CHEESECAKE

Maple Nut Crust:	¼ tsp Sea Salt	4 Tbsp Coconut Oil
1 cup Walnuts	Coconut Oil	4 Tbsp Maple Syrup
½ cup Pecans	*Filling:*	½ cup Coconut Milk
8 Medjool Dates (pitted)	2 cups Cashews	*Topping:*
2 Tbsp Maple Syrup	2 Tbsp Lemon Juice	2 Bosc Pears
	1 Vanilla Bean	Maple Syrup

First, you will need to soak the cashews in water for at least 6 hours, or overnight. This will soften them, ensuring that your cheesecake has a smooth, not gritty, texture.

For the Crust: Preheat the oven to 350 degrees Fahrenheit. Food-process the crust ingredients. If you don't have a food processor, then crush the nuts, mince the dates, and combine all with the remaining crust ingredients.

Press the crust mixture into a greased (with coconut oil) 8" or 9" springform pan, or 3 individual 3" pie pans. We like to use a springform pan, because it makes removing the pie easier, but it isn't imperative. Poke the crust with a fork several times and bake, uncovered, for 12-15 minutes. Watch it at the end, so it doesn't burn. Remove the crust from the heat, and once cool enough, gently press down on the bottom part of the crust, so it really sticks together nicely as it cools.

For the Filling: While the crust is baking and cooling, food-process the cashews, lemon juice, coconut milk, vanilla bean (cut the bean lengthwise, then scrape the insides out with the back side of a knife), coconut oil, and maple syrup until very smooth in texture. Reserve 1 cup for later.

Once the crust is finished, pour the filling into the crust. Evenly spread the mixture out and then place in the freezer while we make the pears.

For the Topping: Preheat the oven to 450 degrees Fahrenheit. Slice the pears to 1/8" thick, spread out on a parchment-lined baking sheet (or greased if you don't have any parchment paper), brush with maple syrup, and roast for 20 minutes, then broil for 5 minutes, or until they are golden brown.

Save several slices of pears for a garnish. Then cut out the seeds, remove the stems and bottoms from the remaining pears, and food-process with the reserved 1 cup filling.

Layer the pear filling on top of the cheesecake filling, decorate the pears on top, and freeze for at least a couple of hours. If frozen overnight or longer, let the cake sit out at room temperature for 30 minutes, then serve.

Tip This recipe tastes great with our Vanilla Bean Ice Cream! (see page 180)

Makes 8" pie

This recipe is Vegan

HONEY MANGO MERINGUE PIE

Crust:	Filling:	Topping:
1 cup Cashews	1 Honey Mango	3 Egg Whites
3 Tbsp Coconut Flour	Juice of 2 Meyer Lemons	1 Tbsp Honey
2 Tbsp Honey	2 Tbsp Honey	1 Vanilla Bean
2 Eggs	2 Eggs	¼ cup Water
2 Tbsp Coconut Oil	1 Egg Yolk	1 Tbsp Arrowroot Powder
⅛ tsp Sea Salt	1 Tbsp Coconut Oil	⅛ tsp Sea Salt

For the Crust: Preheat the oven to 350 degrees Fahrenheit. Combine all crust ingredients in a food processor and blend until smooth. This dough will not be a ball. You will need to gently press the crust mixture into a greased (with coconut oil) 8" or 9" springform pan, or 3 individual 3" pie pans. We like to use a springform pan, because it makes removing the pie easier, but it isn't imperative. Poke the crust with a fork several times and bake, uncovered, for 10–12 minutes. Watch it at the end, so it doesn't burn. Remove the crust from the heat, and once cool enough, gently press down on the bottom part of the crust, so it really sticks together nicely as it cools.

For the Filling: First, skin the mango and cut off the meat. Add the mango pieces and Meyer lemon juice to a food processor or blender and puree, then set aside. Heat the honey and coconut oil in a double boiler over medium-high heat (~7). I would say the double boiler is important, so that the mixture doesn't burn. Once the oil has liquefied, strain the mango puree into it, whisking. Don't let it boil. Once the mango is incorporated, whisk the eggs and egg yolk in a separate bowl and then slowly whisk them into the mango mixture. Turn the heat down to medium (~4) and continue to whisk until set up, which should take about 5–10 minutes. Set aside.

For the Topping: Combine the honey, water, arrowroot powder, vanilla bean (cut the bean lengthwise, then scrape out the insides with the back side of a knife), and sea salt. Set aside. In a bowl, whip the egg whites until soft peaks form. Once you have soft peaks, add the dissolved honey mixture, then whip continuously until stiff peaks form. This is very important. If you don't have a hand mixer, it will take a long time, so be patient.

Now, we assemble the pie. Pour the filling into the pie crust, then spoon the fluffy topping over the filling. However this looks going into the oven is how it will look coming out, so be aware of this.

Broil for 5 minutes, or until the topping is browned and set.

Makes 8" pie

This recipe is Vegetarian